'Jen writes from a deep well of unde[...] over many years the principles she p[...] we need to cultivate to grasp and pro[...] love of God, Jen says our story is our so.. in which seed is placed, to be nurtured and encouraged into the growth of a healthy, strong future. Laced with humour and self-deprecation, Jen writes to all of us, showing us how to be transparent, vulnerable and open to whatever God wants for us. Invariably that includes seasons experiencing the dark night of the soul, yet Jen gently teaches the reader not to be afraid, but to embrace what God is doing. It is from that point, she makes clear, that great freedom comes. It is such freedom that enables us to leave a legacy which lasts far beyond our own lives and into generations to come. This is a powerful and beautiful book.'

Bev Murrill, preacher,
leadership consultant, mentor and author

'From soil and seed to life and legacy, Jen Baker skilfully guides the hopeful heart through the process of waiting for the fulfilment of their developing promise. With deep wisdom, tender instruction, and moments of true grit, Jen's anointed and artful words in *The Power of a Promise* will be a catalyst, inspiring the reader to hold on to the promise of their dream until it becomes reality. A must read for anyone who hopes for the fruition of their potential.'

Dawn Scott Damon, author

'In an easy, "grab-a-coffee and chat" style, Jen uses the illustration of the season of the seed to talk about the power of a promise. Using her own experiences, she writes with humour, honesty and wisdom. A great reminder to cultivate the promises spoken over our own lives. I was gripped reading it and highly recommend this book for those holding onto promises in their own lives.'

Leanne Mallett, National Aspire Leader, Elim

'I know Jen Baker for her passion and authentic approach in life. *The Power of a Promise* is filled with inspiration and will prepare you to stand tall when the odds are against you. Jen's personal experiences of life and adventures on a journey of healing, freedom and truth fill the pages and she captures the art of celebrating who she is, while still believing the best is yet to come. This book makes for a captivating read and even more passion for life!'

Shaneen Clarke, author and international speaker

'God has placed in the heart and mind of all man a dream, a divine design, a promise. Of course, it begins by entering into a deep and abiding relationship with our Creator, through his son Jesus Christ, but far too many have taken this initial step and assumed they have arrived. Nothing could be further from the truth, or a greater waste of the divine gift. Read this book, allow God to speak to your heart and reveal to you the promise he has for your life, and then live every day cultivating that promise in your life and the lives of those around you.'

Jerry Shaffer, pastor, The Well, Geneva, Illinois, USA

'If you dream of taking some time out with a good friend who is also a wise mentor, I recommend curling up with this book and hanging out with Jen. From start to finish, Jen invites you to join her in exploring God's promises in new and insightful ways. You'll love her stories, you will smile, you will stop and think and you will leave with a fuller heart and a renewed faith.'

Cathy Madavan, writer, speaker, author and
member of Spring Harvest Planning Group

'Jen Baker believes that God plants seeds in your life, seeds that will grow and multiply. She shares stories from the Bible and her own experiences that attest to the wonderful ways he cultivates new life. If you need a boost to your faith, don't miss this book.'

Amy Boucher Pye, author and speaker

The
POWER
of a
PROMISE

Nurturing the Seeds of God's Promises
through the Seasons of Life

Jen Baker

Authentic

First published 2018 by Authentic Media Limited,
PO Box 6326, Bletchley, Milton Keynes, MK1 9GG.
authenticmedia.co.uk

British Library Cataloguing in Publication Data
A catalogue record for this book is available from the British Library

ISBN: 978-1-78078-986-6
978-1-78078-987-3 (e-book)

Cover design by Zeljka Kojic
vukojeviczelika@gmail.com

Printed and bound by CPI Group (UK) Ltd., Croydon, CR0 4YY

Copyright Acknowledgements

Contents

Dedicated to
Elaine Miller and Shari McCord
Thank you for letting me be part of the family, the story and the journey.
I love the tapestry of legacy God has created among us.

Acknowledgments

First and foremost I want to thank the Father, Son and Holy Spirit. Knowing you, discovering you, journeying with you and learning from you is truly my greatest joy in life. How is it possible to feel I couldn't know you more, while simultaneously feeling I hardly know you at all? You are the greatest desire of my heart and the love of my life – thank you for all that has been, and all I am unaware is yet to be.

My parents – Bob and Barb Baker. You are my strong foundation and the greatest cheerleaders a girl could ever want. From you I have learned how to love well and live well. I will be forever grateful for both my spiritual heritage and pioneering spirit – learned through watching you. You have given me wings to fly, yet a nest to always call home. Through you I have been free to explore, grow, fall, get up and step out into all that God has called me to be – experiencing first-hand the power of promise fulfilled. Thank you for never giving up on me and loving me as fiercely as you have. I love you.

My siblings – Tammi/Werner and Bobby/Kimi. Thank you for standing with me, sending the encouraging messages, and being the quiet supporters in the background. I know that wherever I am you are with me, and that strengthens my soul on the tough days. I love you.

Dorothy and Hobbes – please don't grow up yet; I adore your cuteness and love you to the moon and back.

Lisa – words aren't enough to express my thanks for all you have done to support me in this journey. Nobody will ever know the hundreds of sacrifices you have made, including bringing me coffee and cleaning my flat because I hadn't left my writing desk in so many days! You are the epitome of a servant of Christ and I know this is only the beginning of unlimited promises breaking forth over your own life – I am standing by and cheering you on as they continue to unfold.

My 'inner circle' – you know who you are. Thank you. Just . . . thank you.

My prayer team and financial partners – you also know who you are. I pray for you daily and love you dearly. Thank you for your support, in so many ways. I could not do this journey without you – and I would not want to.

Amber – you are my oldest friend and longest-standing non-family cheerleader. We have travelled many roads together, faced the perils of Chicago and navigated the challenges of an overseas friendship. Though our lives could not have taken more different paths, we have stood the tests of separation and change – and have overcome. You are precious to my heart and I love you deeply. Thank you for always having a cup of tea ready. You are a true friend.

Bev Murrill – we have journeyed many roads together, my friend. I honour you, love you and am with you as we watch God unfold, yet unseen, promises in both of our lives. Clear away those spiders and I'll come have a coffee with you in Australia.

Laura Ryder – thank you for the cheering and the challenging; the Lord knew I had a Laura-sized space missing in my life.

Jennifer Dykema – thank you for allowing me to share your beautifully written words . . . I am so proud of you. Chase those dreams, sweetheart.

Esther Rudge – because you asked if you were in my book . . . I pray a small part of my legacy will live through you, beautiful girl. I love who you are becoming; keep being marvellous you.

The Authentic Media family – I've only known you for two minutes, but I quite like you already. Donna Harris, thank you for your endless encouragement and constant support; Becky Fawcett and Mollie Barker, thank you for answering my unending questions and for keeping me on track and making me a better writer. And to the many others I don't know by name helping make this book a reality – thank you.

And finally: Amy Boucher Pye, for providing unending wisdom on tap. You make me better – thank you, friend; Cathy Madavan, for making the journey fun and for writing a book at the same time, so I didn't feel so alone – let's go find chocolate to celebrate; Arianna Walker, for that lunch; Isabelle, for being obedient; Sue G. and Susie H. for praying; Facebook friends/community for endless support and encouragement; Maria Rodriguez for being queen of encouragement; Bri for simply being you and making me smile; Jerry Shaffer for hearing from God and sending that text; Dan/Fi and Estienne/Grant for waiting at the door of my next season with open arms and open hearts; and . . . I am so uncomfortable writing a list like this because I am pretty certain I will forget someone. Please forgive me if you are not here and should be.

The reader – *thank you* for doing this journey with me. I pray you enjoy our time together chatting by the imaginary fire. Now, it is your time to shine in the brilliance of all he has promised. Enjoy your seasons.

Introduction

I am not known for my navigational prowess. If I say 'Turn right', please go left immediately.

This gift has benefits, though, not the least presenting many opportunities to explore places I never intended to visit. I have been lost in the city, the country, the hills, the valleys . . . from Italy to Australia to America . . . well, just about any country I have placed my feet. I thank the Lord that I am alive during the age of smartphones – I fear to think how I would have coped in Jesus' day. Surely I would have died from detour dehydration.

Our lives can often feel like my navigational skills – taking us round a bend, over a hill, into dead ends, detours or road construction, leaving us going in circles and quite plainly just a bit clueless about our whereabouts. We can feel inept in negotiating the terrain, hoping we are heading in the right direction, yet underneath wondering if staying in bed would have been the better option.

Playing it safe is the antithesis of discovery – and we were created to discover. As a child after birth immediately begins exploring their surroundings – by sight, sound, taste and touch – so are we to step out of our comfort zones and into our calling, one experience at a time.

Throughout the following pages we will study how Jesus journeyed his own destiny – from before the beginning of time to a legacy which carries on today. He was known in heaven before he was born on earth, and so were you. Jesus changed his world for all of eternity, and so can you. We do not need to change nations; we only need to walk in obedience. Psalm 139:16 esv says: 'Your eyes saw my unformed substance; in your book were written, every one of them, the days that were formed for me, when as yet there was none of them.'

God has a few books, and one of them – according to this scripture – details the days he has ordained for our lives. Days which contain promise and potential, blessing and influence. These days are interspersed within seasons, some challenging and others uplifting, all working to bring about the good promises established for our lives before creation.

By knowing the seasons – and promises – that accompany our journey, we can better navigate where we are currently and where God might be leading us ultimately. The promises from God are always hidden before they are fully heard and seen, yet lack of sight does not indicate lack of substance. They are hidden in his word, giving us opportunity to study and digest, gaining greater understanding as our relationship with him matures. Or they are hidden in his heart, planned for the time when our character is strong enough to maintain that facet of our calling. Our life journey is fluid, not concrete. In other words, we keep moving – like a river – navigating the twists and turns as we go; because time continues, indifferent to our readiness for change. By not mourning yesterday, and not fearing tomorrow, we can embrace our present, watching a loving God navigate a powerful future.

It is the power within a promise which strengthens our grip when we'd rather let go. As an acorn potentially houses an oak tree and as a woman carries seeds of new life, so we spiritually hold seeds of promise over our lives until we see them come to fruition in fullness. God has called some of us to travel to many nations, others to influence our neighbourhood; some he asks to work in government and others to focus on the poor. We each have promises specific to us, plans and purposes uniquely designed for our area of influence. Not one person is born without promise and purpose – not one. Some seeds produce fruit, and others a forest, yet both are vital to the wellbeing and health of the world in which we live.

What does your promise hold?

Our seasons have similarities, though details will vary with each story. Therefore, we will explore six main seasons: soil, seed, growth, life, epoch, legacy. These represent the stages I believe every healthy seed experiences, and the seasons Jesus himself navigated as an example for us all. Each phase has lessons, sorrows, joys and challenges, but as a whole they move us from insignificant and without form, to influencing beyond our lifetime.

As I intersperse my story here and there, I pray you will find your own story throughout the pages. And that you might experience a greater depth of intimacy with God, resulting in a bolder faith and clearer witness.

Most importantly, I pray we will all recognize that our lives still matter, regardless of age or occupation, and that if we are still breathing, there are promises yet to break forth if we refuse to let go.

Promises . . . filled with power.

Part One

Soil

The thief comes only to steal and kill and destroy. I came that they may have life and have it₁ abundantly John 10:10

Prepare the Soil

I came that they may have and enjoy life,
and have it in abundance [to the full, till it
overflows].

John 10:10 AMP

How Rich Is Your Soil?

I tried gardening once. Let me say, 'Thank you, Lord, for florists.'

Then I tried my hand at trimming shrubs – how difficult could it be to trim and maintain a rounded shape?

Difficult.

Nobody could ever mistake me for a horticulturalist, agriculturalist or any other type of 'ist' dealing with foliage. I love the idea of getting my hands dirty in the soil of creation, but unless 'becoming one with nature' includes a manicure, it is not for me.

Despite my lack of gardening knowledge, I have learned this – soil is significant.

You will hear this a few times throughout our time together: bad soil will never reap a good harvest. Because seeds are developed underground, and if they cannot thrive under the earth, they will not survive above the earth. Most of us walk through our everyday lives, never thinking about the *terra firma* beneath our feet. Until writing this book I basically noticed two things about soil: it is either dry or wet. Beyond that my knowledge was sadly lacking. Yet a quick Wikipedia search brought up a plethora of information which was actually fascinating, and surprisingly spiritually relevant.

For example, did you know that the nature of the parent material, or the rock from which the soil is derived, ranks among five key factors influencing the characteristics of soil in a given environment?[1] Me neither. One of the greatest factors in soil is the rock from which it was originally derived. Similarly, whatever constitutes our 'rock' in life will greatly affect the soil in which we place our seeds of promise. If faith is the rock creating the soil of belief in our hearts, then faith-filled soil will surround our hoped-for promise. Alternatively, if wealth, popularity, acceptance or success define the foundation on which we want to build, then the substance of our lives (soil) will be made up of something which is, in the scheme of long-lasting, shallow at best.

Take a moment to consider your rock in life. Is your faith built on a solid foundation or something better described as shifting sand? We know the right answer, yet if we get honest many of us would admit our faith is ultimately placed in the economy, our job, relationships, talents, or other more tangible securities. Imagine how you might respond if one of these areas were to falter. Would your first response be running to God, finding a scripture, declaring the truth and standing on his promises? Or would it be to phone a friend and post the problem across social media?

Remember what Jesus said to Peter in Matthew 16:18 when talking about a solid foundation: 'And I tell you that you are

Peter, and on this rock I will build my church, and the gates of Hades will not overcome it.'

The name Peter means rock or small stone, but the word 'rock' used in the verse above is a *feminine* version of the word, which is interpreted more as a mass of connected rock or a boulder, such as one projecting out of a cliff (as opposed to *Petros* which means a detached mass of rock).[2]

I interpret it as a word symbolizing strength, power, authority and depth. I especially like that it is a feminine definition which exudes strength, power, authority, depth – and connection. All of these are to be incorporated into our daily lives, male or female, with no distinction. It is that image which Jesus declares his church will be built upon; and it is that image on which the rich soil of our faith is formed, ready to receive the promises of God.

Keeping Up Appearances

In Matthew 13 we find one of the best-known parables in the Bible, and it deals with soil:

That same day Jesus went out of the house and sat beside the sea. And great crowds gathered about him, so that he got into a boat and sat down. And the whole crowd stood on the beach. And he told them many things in parables, saying: 'A sower went out to sow. And as he sowed, some seeds fell along the path, and the birds came and devoured them. Other seeds fell on rocky ground, where they did not have much soil, and immediately they sprang up, since they had no depth of soil, but when the sun rose they were scorched. And since they had no root, they withered away. Other seeds fell among thorns, and the thorns grew up and choked them. Other seeds fell on good soil and produced grain, some a hundredfold, some sixty, some thirty. He who has ears, let him hear.'

Matt. 13:1–9 ESV

We see here that seed is carrying within it the potential to produce abundance, but the soil provides the appropriate environment for that seed to take root and begin growing. It is meant to provide a safe home for transformation to happen, by protecting, feeding and enriching the vulnerable seed within its borders. If that seed does not take root, what could have been will never see the light of day.

The same can happen in our own lives. We have seeds of promise, prophetic words, personal dreams and desires, but if they are not planted in the strong soil of faith, truth, prayer and God's word then we give opportunity for the enemy to steal what is not rightfully his to keep. Even when the enemy interferes, as he will always try to do, God has the final say and his ways will be 'beyond anything we can dream or even imagine' (see Eph. 3:20). I have seen that happen innumerable times in my life; he is simply too good to be stopped by a defeated foe!

I can also say, with tremendous conviction, that the soil of my heart has proven to be the greenhouse or slaughterhouse for any potential promise or future harvest. When my heart has been filled with self-pity, anger, bitterness, unforgiveness and insecurity (personalize your own list here), seeds of budding promise have struggled to survive, as the environment of my heart was not conducive to growth, only death. We are all on our own journey of faith and there is no condemnation implied or insinuated, but let me be abundantly clear at the start – without rich soil there cannot be a pure, abundant harvest. Because it is not about looking good outwardly; it is about being rich inwardly.

We only need to study Christ to see this. He was a 'seed' planted thousands of years before his arrival, spoken through the prophets and awaited by the generations . . . yet his appearance was nothing worthy of a double take. He could have been described as ordinary; remember those who said 'Isn't this Joseph's son?' (e.g. Luke 4:22), astonished that one so ordinary could be creating the extraordinary.

This is the call of God on all our lives. God does not create ordinary and we are not, at our core, natural. He dwells with the ordinary, but where his presence and power are active we will always find extraordinary and supernatural. Try and find a place in the Bible where people were seeking truth, God showed up . . . and things stayed as they were. It didn't happen! Scripture says that in Nazareth Jesus could do no miracles, but that was due to lack of faith – not lack of power. From Pentecost in Acts 2 to the return of Christ in the book of Revelation, his presence changed atmospheres.

And in the same way, he has not created us to be ordinary, boring, carrying on the best they can, simply persevering through life until we die. What an awful God that would be if that were true. I would never follow a god like that. No, he has created us unique, one-of-a-kind, born to impact this world for his kingdom – all of us. Yet when we live below his best, consumed with fitting into a world which doesn't fit the kingdom, then we are left with only a shallow depth of soil hardly able to sustain the life of a seed destined for impact. This is not God's best, nor will, for his children.

> He has created us unique, one-of-a-kind, born to impact this world for his kingdom.

We will delve further into this in the next chapter, but I encourage us at this early stage to, quite bluntly, let the Holy Spirit begin digging around in our dirt.

Perhaps pause right now and give him permission to begin turning up the spotlight over your heart as you continue with the book?

Go ahead . . . I'll wait.

Living in the Overflow

At the beginning of the chapter we see the Amplified Bible describing the kind of life that Jesus brings: it is abundant 'to the full, till it overflows' (John 10:10).

Have you ever stood near Niagara Falls in Ontario, Canada? Or near any other mighty rushing river? The sound is deafening and the power overwhelming – enough so that even with barriers people stand back from the edge, not taking any chances of experiencing that overflow up close and personal! I believe that picture beautifully represents the overflowing life of God roaring on the inside of us.

The Greek word for power used over 120 times in the New Testament is *dunamis*. It is defined in part as 'physical power, force, might, ability, efficacy, energy, powerful deeds, marvellous works'. An online biblical word-study explains it as 'the ability to perform' or 'power through God's ability'.[3] This is the same word used in Acts 1:8 ESV where the risen Jesus says: 'But you will receive power when the Holy Spirit has come upon you, and you will be my witnesses in Jerusalem and in all Judea and Samaria, and to the end of the earth.'

It is also the same word used at the beginning of Ephesians 1:19–20 ESV where the apostle Paul describes 'the immeasurable greatness of [God's] power towards us who believe, according to the working of his great might that he worked in Christ when he raised him from the dead and seated him at his right hand in the heavenly places'.

Again, it is his power (*dunamis*), available for believers, which is strong enough to perform miracles such as raising Christ from the dead and seating him at the right hand of the Father. That exact power dwells right now on the inside of all believers. *Right now.* Yet, how often have we seen our circumstances through the eyes of defeat and smallness, instead of the eyes of victory and greatness?

> His power is not dependent on our ability; our ability is dependent on his power.

His power is not dependent on our ability; our ability is dependent on his power.

Maintaining that order keeps us balanced between humility and authority, and between humanity and righteousness. As we intentionally focus on the indwelling power of God, we can begin to see our lives through his eyes – free, powerful and filled with purpose. Once we not only acknowledge this power, but deliberately act from this power, we will begin to see a dramatic change in our outlook, circumstances and belief system. More will be said about this in chapter three, but for now let me say: we cannot overflow what is not already flowing.

Soil Content

You may have guessed by now that I'm not a soil expert (that is a gross understatement), but one thing I do know is that soil differs in various climates and countries. Think of the red soil of the Grand Canyon compared to the lush soil of California's Great Central Valley (yes, I had to google that). Soil tells a story, as does our lives.

I grew up in the midwestern United States, moving to England in my early thirties. At the time of this writing I have lived in the UK for fourteen years, have obtained dual citizenship, adopted the term AmeriBrit and developed an intense love for both nations. My American accent has softened a bit, and due to frequent travel, I am regularly asked the question 'Where are you from?' I never quite know how to answer that. Do they mean the city I live in now or the country where I was born? Are they speaking about my identity as an American, as a Brit or as an everyday human being? I think even for people rooted and grounded in one location for most of their lives, the question of 'Who am I?' or 'Where do I belong?' is never far from their hearts, until they find home in a relationship with their Creator.

It is only in turning to Christ that we find ourselves totally at home, fully accepted and intrinsically aligned for purpose. Our story is essentially our soil. For me, copious amounts of moving, never feeling like I fitted in and a shocking amount of insecurity led me to seek what identity looked like from a heavenly perspective. What I have learned is being written in another book, but for now let me say that knowing our identity in Christ creates a kingdom confidence, one which far surpasses earthly confidence. And it is within kingdom confidence that our soil is richest for growing seeds of promise.

As you continue reading this book, I pray the Holy Spirit will begin untangling any intruder which has wrapped itself around the soil of your heart. For you were created to be brave, stand the test of time and overcome by his overcoming power within you.

For reflection

- What, or who, would you define as the foundation of your life and how is this played out practically? Has this changed over the years?

- As you let the Lord begin 'digging in your dirt' so to speak, do you think he would find seeds on the path, in rocky soil or amongst the thorns? What percentage of your seeds (promises) do you think he would find in good soil?

- I speak about being created to do the extraordinary because, at our core, we are supernatural beings. How do you feel about that thought in relation to your life? Where have you seen God do the extraordinary?

- *'His power is not dependent on our ability; our ability is dependent on his power.'* Where have you tried to walk in your own power or ability instead of trusting God to work his power through you? What were the results?

2

Beware of the Enemy

The thief comes only in order to steal and kill and destroy.

John 10:10 AMP

Fine, I'll Move!

'But, Lord, I don't *waaaant* to leave!' I whined.

Many years ago I was renting a flat on the lovely south coast of Devon, England, when God made it quite clear he was moving me, against my will, to the bustling city of London.

It was now two weeks before the move date and I had yet to pack a single item – I was in full-blown rebellion and he knew it. I can never prove it was God who orchestrated the next turn of events, but I am wholly convinced it was.

After moaning daily about not wanting to leave my seaside flat (OK, you could see a tiny corner of the sea if you stood on the sofa), I arrived home one night to what can only be described as my worst nightmare. Walking into my bedroom and beginning to prepare for bed, I turned around to find a gigantic (I am not exaggerating) spider on my pillow – sprawled out like he was sunning himself along the French Riviera. He might as well have had a martini in hand and grapes being fed to him the way he reclined on what, to him, was an enormous marshmallow. As spiders are my second worst fear (solidly placed behind sharks) I nearly went into cardiac arrest when, backing away from the bed towards the window, I turned in time to avoid a backside squeeze from another massive spider abseiling the curtains behind me.

'*Jeessuusss!*' was all I could scream.

I quickly reminded him I had no husband, therefore this was *his* responsibility. I am sure I could hear heaven laughing. Suddenly I had a strong sense the Lord was asking me if I was ready to move yet? I started packing that night.

Fear (or any attack of the enemy for that matter) moves us. We decide in which way it will move us, but, trust me, it will move us one way or another – into growing deeper roots of trust or, alternatively, uprooting potential seeds of promise: the choice is ours.

What Do You Believe?

I don't think many people believe we can simply coast through life, wait on God, take no initiative and expect to live an overflowing, powerful life. And if you do believe that, I'm sorry to burst your bubble, but please re-enter the real world! As wonderful as life is, and it is, it also brings with it difficulties, challenges, surprises and obstacles to overcome. Coasting is simply not an option for those who want to live the kingdom life.

We know that God has not given us a spirit of fear (2 Tim. 1:7), therefore fear is of the enemy, and because he is the father of all lies, what we fear will be filled with fabrication.

Yes, those spiders could have potentially crawled on me. But they were not going to do what my imagination saw them doing: leap on me (why do we assume all spiders are long-jumpers?) and methodically gnaw me for a late-night snack.

In Christ, faith obliterates what fear exaggerates.

The bottom line is this: where is our faith and what do we believe? Let's look again at our scripture from the last chapter:

> That same day Jesus went out of the house and sat beside the sea. And great crowds gathered about him, so that he got into a boat and sat down. And the whole crowd stood on the beach. And he told them many things in parables, saying: 'A sower went out to sow. And as he sowed, some seeds fell along the path, and the birds came and devoured them. Other seeds fell on rocky ground, where they did not have much soil, and immediately they sprang up, since they had no depth of soil, but when the sun rose they were scorched. And since they had no root, they withered away. Other seeds fell among thorns, and the thorns grew up and choked them. Other seeds fell on good soil and produced grain, some a hundredfold, some sixty, some thirty. He who has ears, let him hear.'
>
> Matt. 13:1–9 ESV

The first example we see of seed being stolen was it falling along the path, never taking root. This is where belief comes to assist – it helps the promises of God to take root within the soil of our hearts. When a promise is left to sit on the path of 'God might and God might not', or 'I hope this will work', or 'God is punishing me', or any other unhelpful sayings which have become familiar platitudes, it stops the promise from taking root in healthy soil and instead leaves it vulnerable to the enemy of our soul.

mindset in western society today, and I believe it is an attitude infiltrating the wider church, to its detriment. I have nothing against mega-churches, loud music or thousands of people gathering to worship Christ – that's a glimpse of heaven!

But I do have an issue with those who venerate that type of Christianity over the small group meetings in developing countries, where two or three are gathered, praying for one another. That is also a glimpse of heaven. And the moment we think one is greater than another is the moment we have bought into a lie of the enemy, basing acceptance on the world's standards and not heaven's approval.

Time is beautiful. It allows roots to grow deep into the soil, able to withstand the tribulation and persecution that comes with new growth and purposed living. We must stop comparing our achievements with the apparent success of another; this is our race to run and soil to till, not theirs. We must give God time to develop what he wants developing in our lives right now. I believe names we have never heard of will be some of the most celebrated in heaven. An elderly woman who can't walk well, but prays for hours in her bedroom. The African widow ministering to the Muslim neighbour. A little Indian boy who showed love to those who were persecuting him. We must never – ever – compare our lives with what the world deems great. The minute we do, we have bought into an enemy mindset, because the Bible is clear that Satan is the god of this world (2 Cor. 4:4), we are not of this world (John 15:19) and through Christ we have overcome the world (1 John 5:4). So, why would we choose to act according to what we have been set free to overcome?

I am not insinuating that everything we are believing for must be grown in the greenhouse of time; God sometimes moves quickly and does miracles instantaneously. But in my own life I have seen that the majority of 'instant' miracles were actually years in the making; I was simply unaware of God working behind the scenes. And then at the right time he chose to bless me with an answer before I even knew there was a question.

Yet, more often than not, he asks us to fertilize the soil of our faith so the seeds of promise will hold strong, regardless of what comes at them above ground. Depth is always more important to God than display. You may have heard of the giant sequoia trees in California. They are some of the largest trees in the world, yet see how long it's taken for them to grow:

> Depth is always more important to God than display.

> Giant sequoias can grow to be about 30 feet (9 meters) in diameter and more than 250 feet (76 m) tall. The biggest of these behemoths is General Sherman, a giant sequoia in Sequoia National Park. General Sherman stands 275 feet (84 m) tall, has a 102-foot (31 m) circumference, and weighs an incredible 2.7 million lbs. (1.2 million kilograms). Giant sequoias can live to 3,000 years, with the oldest on record living more than 3,500 years.[2]

That is a long time to mature (stating the obvious), but the end product was certainly worth the wait. Reaching unexpected heights, and walking in unforeseen strength, comes from enduring many different seasons. Don't despair if you feel a longed-for promise is late in coming. God sees; he always sees. And he is never short of an answer or a plan . . . even at our midnight hour.

Cast Your Cares

We have seen the enemies of unbelief, persecution and delay which threatened the promised seed, yet the nemesis I believe most vile and prolific in our lives is the last one – thorns. Matthew 13:22 ESV presents thorns as the 'cares of the world and the deceitfulness of riches' – that which weighs us down and leads us astray. In the world in which we live, anxiety and money are two of the greatest thieves of promise fulfilled. I am convinced it is possible to live without the weight of anxiety and cares in our lives; I am not there yet, but I do believe it is possible! Because in 1 Peter 5:7 the apostle exhorts us to 'cast all your anxiety on [God] because he cares for you'. He would not ask us to do something which was not possible to do, therefore a grace to cast our cares must be present.

It is interesting to me that the verse about casting our cares lies in-between a verse above talking about humility and one below referencing an enemy. In-between laying down our lives (v. 6) and facing our enemy (v. 8), we are asked to cast our cares. One would think this scripture might exhort us to be strong, protect and believe in ourselves – words society might use today – yet it says the exact opposite: release your cares to the one who carries that care with ease. By turning loose our cares, we become empowered to live by faith in the one who shows us exactly how to navigate the line between pride and persecution. Yet, by holding on to cares, worry, anxiety and unanswered questions, we allow the potential of promise to be choked by thorns. The last part of Matthew 13:22 says the seed becomes unfruitful. In other words, purpose is aborted and influence is cut short. It is a very sad picture indeed – one I recently discerned in my own life.

Not long ago I was praying with someone and the Lord revealed to me that I was carrying an enormous amount of false responsibility. I believe this stemmed from when I was much younger, riding in the car with my mom and sister. There was typical family tension between a mother and her young children, when I suddenly had this thought pop into my mind: *Jen, make them laugh. It is your responsibility to keep the family happy.*

From that moment forward I intentionally accepted responsibility for keeping everyone happy . . . and eventually it escalated from my family, to friends, to crowds. Public speaking or preaching is an extremely vulnerable profession for one who feeds on the approval of others. And for years I would fight the need to have people tell me how amazing I was after speaking; from doing the announcements to preaching a sermon, I craved the approval of others. Clearly, this is a recipe for disaster for one called to a speaking ministry. The Lord used this prayer ministry to reveal that I was carrying the weight of approval on my shoulders. Inwardly I desired the approval of heaven, but outwardly I sought the acceptance of people.

The wise woman I was praying with said to me, 'Jen, you are called to shift atmospheres when you preach. The enemy started when you were young trying to convince you it was *your* responsibility to shift the atmosphere in that car, therefore you've grown up feeling responsible for whether or not a shift takes place.'[3] And I saw it. The responsibility (care) I had carried was choking the life out of the seed of my potential. If I spent my life worrying about whether or not people liked my message, I would never be fully free to follow the Spirit's leading, regardless of the opinion of others.

I repented.

And I will never forget the freedom and joy in my spirit as I walked into a supermarket[4] on my way home. I looked at the people and thought to myself, *I'm not responsible for you, or you . . . or any of you!* Jesus says (in *The Message*):

Are you tired? Worn out? Burned out on religion? Come to me. Get away with me and you'll recover your life. I'll show you how

For reflection

- Are there any seeds of promise you have left (now or in the past) on the pathway of doubt?

- Have you ever experienced God using an attack of the enemy to move you into position for a blessing? During those seasons, what has God grown in your own heart in relation to character, not comfort?

- Would you agree that anxiety and money are two of the greatest cares people carry with them? What keys have you learned to help you cast those cares onto the Lord, and not take them back again?

- Ask the Holy Spirit to show you if you are taking on a responsibility that belongs to God and/or asking God to take on a responsibility that belongs to you. God never forces us to do anything; the enemy pushes, but God leads.

3

The Power of the Blessing

*If you belong to Christ, then you are Abraham's
seed, and heirs according to the promise.*

Gal. 3:29

Behind the Scenes

By the time I was three years old I had mastered the pout.

My bottom lip was always on standby and within a moment's notice it could march forward, stand to attention, and defend self-pity till its dying breath. I was the younger sibling and it was always on high alert with my sister around, as competition only fuelled its fury. So, when our family fishing trip to Wisconsin found my sister and me standing on the dock fishing with our father, I was prepared.

I gave it time, fixing my eyes on the tiny, wobbling bobber underneath my watchful gaze, just waiting for my bite. This was my time; I could feel it.

'I got one!' I heard my sister yell. I ignored her and stared harder at my bobber, willing it to go under the water.

A few minutes later I heard her squeal 'I got one!'

Not long after, she cheerfully exclaimed 'Daddy, I got another one!'

Life was not going according to my three-year-old plan. Putting down my pole I walked over to peruse her haul of fish. I couldn't believe it – she was catching all my fish.

Pout time.

Looking up at my father I adamantly declared 'I can't do it' . . . lip wide enough for a seagull landing.

'Just try again,' my father suggested while busying himself around me.

Head down, pout out, I declared: 'No, it won't work – she's catching all my fish!'

Kneeling down to my level, my father gently said once again, 'Just try one more time. I bet this time you'll catch something . . .'

Looking into his smiling eyes I gently took his hand, walked to the pole he handed me and tried again. Time stood still as I looked down to see – my bobber had disappeared! I glanced up at my father, who smiled and said, 'Well, go on then – pull it up!'

At that moment my sister could have had a ship full of fish – I didn't care. I had finally caught . . . my fish.

(Fast forward thirteen years.)

Our family was sitting around at dinner time and we began talking about that family holiday and fishing together. I nonchalantly mentioned the fish I had finally caught after so many tries and how pleased I was with my catch. Suddenly I noticed the dinner table grow quiet, stolen glances moving between my sister/mom/dad. Finally I heard my dad gently say, 'I thought you knew.'

'Knew what?' I asked while chewing my dinner.

'*Ummm* . . . well . . . you see . . . I . . . well, your sister had so many fish that when your back was turned I just reached over and . . .'

(Insert time standing still.)

'All these years I've been catching . . . my sister's fish!' I shrieked.

The phrase 'bubble bursting' was made for moments like that.

But one day as I was preparing a message, the Lord brought that (still bruised) memory to mind, and gently showed me the Father's heart. I saw that it was my father's idea to go fishing, therefore my father would do whatever necessary to bring about the desire of his little girl's heart, because it was also his desire for her. And I realized my heavenly Father will work behind the scenes, doing whatever he needs to do, in order to bring about the desires he has planned for my life, using the abundance of others when necessary, knowing that in the future I would be the one sharing the harvest.

The Blessing

The blessing of the promised fish that day reminds me of Jesus telling Peter to pay his taxes by casting his hook and bringing in the first fish he catches, for the money he needed would be in the mouth of the fish (Matt. 17:24–27). I imagine Jesus grinning from ear to ear as he watched Peter give him a 'You're kidding, right?' look, just before hauling in the miraculous provision. God's ways are truly beyond ours, and his possibilities are endless when it comes to provision and blessing. As we close out this chapter I want to remind us of our heritage in Christ, because it is within that heritage that the power of our promises begins taking root.

Deuteronomy 28 is a well-known chapter on the blessings of God. It outlines what we can expect if we walk in obedience to the Lord and his word, things such as blessing over our homes, finances, health and families. Of course, we live in a fallen world and, as we have seen, the enemy will always be there to steal, kill and destroy the intended blessing, but there is a blessing God longs to give us regardless. Proverbs 10:22 ESV says: 'The blessing of the LORD makes rich, and he adds no sorrow with it.'

> 'The blessing of the LORD makes rich, and he adds no sorrow with it' (Prov. 10:22 ESV).

The first words God spoke to Adam and Eve were a blessing as he told them to 'multiply' (see Gen. 1:28). After the flood we see the same words when God blessed Noah and said his family were to 'be fruitful and increase in number' (Gen. 9:1). And there are many more scriptures we could add here; in summary: God loves to bless!

One of the best-known passages on blessing is found a few chapters later in Genesis 12:1–3:

The LORD had said to Abram, 'Go from your country, your people and your father's household to the land I will show you. I will make you into a great nation, and I will bless you; I will make your name great, and you will be a blessing. I will bless those who bless you, and whoever curses you I will curse; and all peoples on earth will be blessed through you.'

Galatians 3:16 says: 'The promises were spoken to Abraham and to his seed. Scripture does not say "and to seeds", meaning many people, but "and to your seed", meaning one person, who is Christ.' If Christ was Abraham's seed, and if we are in Christ, then we are heirs of all the blessings he received. We see this in Galatians 3:29 of the New Testament: 'If you belong to Christ, then you are Abraham's seed, and heirs according to the promise.'

I remember when this truth first started to resonate in my spirit and I grabbed hold of it, not by looking at my circumstances for confirmation, but rather looking at God's word for clarification, of how he intended me to live – the result was clearly blessed and as a blessing. Like any good father, God loves to bless his children, but he also expects his children to be like their heavenly Father, blessing the world around them. Abraham waited for twenty-five years to see his blessing begin to take shape, Jesus waited for thirty years to begin his ministry and we might need to wait even longer for our desired dreams to become reality. Yet both saw their promise fulfilled and blessing multiplied to the next generation – this is our heritage as believers in Christ.

So . . . How's Your Heart?

The first part of this book has intentionally focused on cultivating a rich, fortified soil because, as I have said several times for emphasis, without good soil you will not reap a strong harvest – naturally or spiritually. We all have seeds of promise given to us, both generally in the word and more specifically through our unique purpose, and as we begin exploring the process those seeds undergo to bring forth life, we must first be honest about the soil of our hearts.

As much as the Lord wants to bless us – and he does – he cannot bless disobedience. And it would be unfair to speak about a rich heritage without being honest about the consequences of a disobedient heart. Staying in line with our theme of the seed, we read in Galatians 6:7: 'Do not be deceived: God cannot be mocked. A man reaps what he sows.' We cannot sow to the flesh and expect to reap in the Spirit. It is simply impossible. So, let's take a moment for an honest inventory of our hearts.

I would be remiss if I didn't say upfront that above all, the key to rich soil is a strong, personal relationship with Jesus Christ. He is the one who makes life worth living. I grew up knowing about him, but I didn't realize I could know him personally, as a friend, for many years. I remember the day I finally chose to surrender my life, goals and dreams to him; it was the best decision of my life. I was a Resident Assistant at my university, which meant that I was in charge of a group of girls a year younger than me in their halls of residence.[1] Soon after they arrived I discovered most of them were Christians, and as I was studying for a degree in theatre, I created my own theatre assignment – to convince them I too was a Christian. I like to tell people I lied my way into Christianity.

> The key to rich soil is a strong, personal relationship with Jesus Christ.

As the weeks went by and I 'faked' my Christianity, I found myself becoming more and more interested. So, one day when walking with one of the girls, I casually asked how she would help someone become a Christian, taking mental notes as she talked. A few days later, alone in my bedroom, I gave God my name/birthdate/address/phone number (I assumed Jen Baker was a common name, so he might need some assistance finding the right one) . . . and waited sixty seconds for him to find me across the universal divide. After that it became a bit of a blur as I fumbled my way through a prayer, feeling like a fool and finally squeaking out an amen. I asked him to clarify that he had heard me by releasing a bit of lightning into the sky – lightning seemed like a 'God-tool' he would have on standby.

Nothing happened. I felt even more foolish. So, I got angry, swore like a sailor and went to bed thinking it was all a load of rubbish. Two weeks later I had a horrible day, decided to pick up a Bible . . . and haven't put it down since. The first time I read the Bible I realized *something* had changed, though I could not verbalize what. All I knew was that I experienced a peace inside I had not felt before and that I could have sat and read the word for hours. It was as if a veil had been removed and I could see clearly for the first time in my life. I have told the Lord numerous times that 'my life is not my own', and he knows I mean it.

It was on that basis that I sold everything, moved countries, overcame fears, stood on platforms, wrote books and followed the cloud multiple times to new locations and fresh assignments. What a journey it has been, full of promises – some fulfilled and some I am still holding near my heart thirty years later, wondering if they will ever come to pass.

Whether the promise has been received or is still in the waiting room, I continue to believe, because I have learned that it is daily decisions such as that which decide the direction of my future.

So, how much access to your heart does God have? Are there any rooms he is not allowed to enter? Richness of relationship is what ultimately grows richness of soil, producing the best environment for promises to be grown. He is a gentleman and will never push his way into our hearts, but at an invitation he will move in with grace, peace and love – one step at a time.

If you desire to become a Christian, or to re-dedicate your life to Christ, please see the prayer in the 'Author's Note' at the end of the book. I promise, inviting him in to your heart is the best decision you could ever make.

For reflection

- How do you feel knowing that God *desires* to bless you? How has he tangibly shown you those blessings over the years? (Take some time to give him praise and thanksgiving!)

- What seeds are you choosing to plant into good soil today? What kind of harvest are you believing to see?

- At the end of this chapter I asked: how much access to your heart does God have? How would you answer that question?

  If you have never prayed to receive Christ, or perhaps have walked away from the faith, I would encourage you to pray the salvation prayer found in the Author's Note. And then please send me an email and let me know so that I can rejoice with you!

4

Cultivating Rich Soil

*And we know that all things work together for
good to them that love God, to them who are the
called according to his purpose.*

Rom. 8:28 KJV

The Power of Intention

For years I said that I would never run a marathon.

I mean, let's be honest, choosing to run 26.2 miles in one go –
who in their right mind does that? But in one acute moment
of insanity I went online, filled out a form and voluntarily
declared my intent to run for several torturous hours around
the city of London.

It was a strange mix of sorrow and elation when I received
news that I hadn't made the ballot, or any of my chosen
charities. My marathon dream was over before it had even
begun and, instead of training with intense mileage for the first
half of the year, I continued my gentle saunters of 4 miles a few
times every week. My theory: why push myself when there was
no need? Yet I was about to discover that training (pushing)
isn't for our current season as much as for our future season.

Nine weeks before the marathon I received a phone call from the Alzheimer's Society asking if I would take the place of someone who had to pull out of the race – and, by the way, they needed an answer within two hours. Nine weeks to train for a marathon . . . two hours to decide? Sporty friends of mine discouraged it, but I sensed the Lord confirming this was him, so I agreed.

Then I panicked.

I increased my training runs from 4 miles to 8 miles within a week, surprised that I was able to double my distance in such a short amount of time. The Lord reminded me that I had been in training for nearly twenty years – I just hadn't known it. Running consistently for many years, even for short distances, created a foundation that was easy to build upon. Within a few more weeks I was regularly running over 10 miles and on 22 April 2012 I ran 26.2 miles in 4 hours, 53 minutes and 36 seconds! One of my most painful experiences (which you'll hear about later), yet equally one of my most exhilarating.

I learned a valuable lesson through that experience: little choices matter a great deal. What seemed minimal became monumental at the time I needed it most. As it says in Zechariah 4:10 NLT: 'Do not despise these small beginnings'.

Worm Power

As it does in the spiritual realm, cultivating rich soil in the natural realm takes effort and intentionality. We have seen how small choices make a large difference physically; small creatures equally make an enormous impact naturally. I am talking about our friend, the worm.

In the natural world, worms, work and water are some of the key essentials to healthy soil. When all three are working together properly, they increase the chances of rich soil bringing a great harvest in season. Let's take a look at worms for a moment. Though I grew up a country girl, now that I am older I relate more to the city lifestyle – much to my father's chagrin. I like to think I'm biblical – started in a garden, ends in a city . . .

But one of my favourite days every year is when I get to go fishing with my dad on the lake. Living in England means I have extremely limited family time, so these days are precious for a number of reasons. And regardless of how I feel towards them, worms are essential to the success of our fishing expedition. In doing research for this book I've learned something interesting about these legless, wiggly creatures: they are also extremely important to the richness of soil.

When an animal or plant dies, the complex substances it contains are not in a form that could be used by a nearby plant and the remains are distasteful to most animals. However, our friend the earthworm, having a keen taste for decomposing plant and animal life, eagerly consumes what others would leave behind. The complex chemicals in their digestive system cause a chemical reaction with their food. Due to God's amazing ingenuity, the earthworm is an organism which has the ability to break down the enzymes and proteins in the dead animal or plant material making them once again viable nutrients for nourishing plants and enriching the soil underneath our feet.[1] Amazing.

In simpler language, decay and – let's be blunt – worm poo are critical to the development of rich soil, which creates an environment for healthy growth. And so it is in our lives.

What seems like, or actually is, an area of breakdown in our lives can miraculously be turned around for something good; and it is often that which presents itself as 'manure' which, if we allow it, releases the promise of our future. I would even go so far as to say that if released to God it is *guaranteed* to turn into something good, because that is simply the way he works. If we refuse to give up and choose to wait on the Lord's timing, the enemy cannot win against a God whose intention is love.

> The enemy cannot win against a God whose intention is love.

But as I alluded to in my opening story, we must make intentional choices to assist in fruitful outcomes, as we will see next.

The Lowlands

As much as we like to be on the mountaintops of life, it is often the lowlands where real transformation takes place and, not surprisingly, it is the same with soil. Reading up a bit on topography, I discovered that the process of erosion (by wind, water, glaciers, etc.) will often result in soil and organic matter being moved from higher ground downwards until it eventually reaches the valley bottoms. For this reason, it is usually the lowlands which are more fertile than the beautiful mountaintops which might be overshadowing them.[2]

> As much as we like to be on the mountaintops of life, it is often the lowlands where real transformation takes place.

The richest of soil is found in the lowest of places; while mountaintops are indeed beautiful, they cannot produce rich vegetation or abundant foliage. Equally, I have found it was after my lowest seasons that I experienced my greatest breakthroughs. We do not have to read far in Scripture before we see this as a spiritual truth throughout the Bible. Joseph grew his leadership skills while being stuck in prison; Esther emerged as a powerful queen after first facing her greatest fears; Peter denied his Lord in cowardly fashion before boldly shaping church history; and Jesus faced his own agonizing death before rising to bring eternal life.

I have learned not to desire difficult seasons, but to embrace them. Because I know, if pressed in to God, that season will become a defining moment of my character development. I cannot explain it, but I have seen that when a gift I carry is metaphorically put on the shelf, that same gift goes to a new level of anointing once I use it again. For example, years ago I was a sign-language interpreter for the deaf, and due to a location move I went without interpreting for many months. After, at least, six months of limited use, I was asked to step in for someone at the last moment – actually, in the middle of a sermon! I'll never forget sitting down and watching as concepts and signs began flying out of my fingers at a rate I didn't know that I knew. It was a supernatural touch of God, which never left for many years, and which prepared me to take over leadership of that particular ministry after a short space of time. Within moments I went from shelf-sitting to promotion, and so can you. I realize it is difficult, but if you feel a particular part of your life is on the shelf, don't despair. Instead, increase your faith to believe for promotion, at the right time and within the right environment. Trust me, it is God's speciality.

Seasons of time off, difficulty or 'lowlands' are absolutely rich with nutrients of wisdom, experience and knowledge needed for our next season. Perhaps this is a season of stepping aside and resting, in order to enrich the soil of your future promotion. Don't fight the season; if it seems all doors are closing and the way forward is fog-covered, then I would encourage you to rest until the way becomes clear. By resting I do not mean becoming spiritually lethargic; I mean not striving to find an answer or force a way. Allow this time to saturate yourself in the word of God and worship of God, listen for the still, small voice and rest in the knowledge that he will never leave you nor forsake you and that his ways are far greater than what you can see right now.

Ask him for treasures in the waiting and then look for what he sends you; you will see his blessing in small, and large, ways that will surprise you and strengthen your faith for the next season. Most importantly, never – ever – stop believing by faith.

Living Water

In chapter one I mentioned overflowing from what is already flowing; in other words, something cannot overflow what it does not already contain. I find it fascinating that, depending on our age, the percentage of water in our bodies is 50–75%. At least half of what makes us who we are is water. Without it we will die; a person can go at least three weeks with no food, but is limited to a week, at most, surviving without water. So, if we know our physical bodies need to be watered, and we know that actual soil needs to be regularly watered for plants to thrive (ask me how I know), why would we think spiritually we can survive without the water of the word (Eph. 5:26), which we are told is necessary for a healthy church, and the power of the Holy Spirit, which is flowing within every believer?

One of the best-known stories in the New Testament is in John 4 where we find a Samaritan woman chatting to Jesus at a well. She had come for physical water, but Jesus began speaking of living water. She immediately asked for this water, and then he gently confronted her on her history of previous marriages. Trying to deflect the conversation, she rapidly moved it from water to worship, talking to him about worshipping on the nearby mountain. Maybe if Jesus got distracted by the scenery he might forget her brokenness? It was then Jesus explained that true worshippers worship the Father in spirit and in truth. In other words, there was a spiritual water which could satisfy even the driest of thirst.

John 7:37–39 says:

> On the last and greatest day of the festival, Jesus stood and said in a loud voice, 'Let anyone who is thirsty come to me and drink. Whoever believes in me, as Scripture has said, rivers of living water will flow from within them.' By this he meant the Spirit, whom those who believed in him were later to receive. Up to that time the Spirit had not been given, since Jesus had not yet been glorified.

Bluntly put, it is impossible to cultivate rich soil and to be all Christ died for us to be if we read our Bibles, yet refuse to spend time in his presence, and especially with the Holy Spirit. He is a gift given to us, and regardless of our theological leaning (e.g. to speak in tongues or not to speak in tongues) the Holy Spirit is the one Jesus left with us to guide us into all truth and enable us to walk through life victoriously in this world. I'll be honest: when I first became a Christian I was comfortable with Jesus, afraid of the Father, and really wanted nothing to do with the Holy Spirit – in my book he was too weird. There isn't space here to detail my journey, but suffice to say the Lord was gracious and took me where I was, until I was comfortable meeting him where he wanted me to be. Once I discovered more of the Father's love, I was freed to explore who the Holy Spirit was for me.

I remember asking him one day to show me – gently – and with no weirdness – who he was. It has been the most beautiful journey and one that I will always cherish. He is my counsellor, my guide, my wisdom, my reminder of all the things I'm forgetting to do, my friend, my joy, my laughter . . . I simply cannot imagine my life without him in it! I am so grateful I intentionally focused on getting to know him; my connection with heaven and spiritual maturity has grown in leaps and bounds the more I have spent time with him, prayed in the Spirit, read about him and asked for his guidance. He is often the one I greet first thing in the morning and the one I converse with throughout the day; he truly has become a best friend.

If this is new territory for you, I would invite you to seek him out yourself. Begin reading about the Spirit in the Scriptures, ask him to gently reveal himself to you, and ask him more often for help – from understanding the Bible to remembering where you put your car keys. He is such a joy. And as you take intentional, small steps to water yourself with the word and the Holy Spirit, you will find the soil of your heart getting cultivated to a new level – one able to go the distance.

Finally, as you continue reading I want you to imagine we are friends, chatting over coffee next to a crackling fireplace. As we progress I will share more strands of my story, juxtaposed with Christ's story, believing for your story to intertwine with ours throughout the pages. Because in the kingdom of God

For reflection

- Do you believe the sentence: '*The enemy cannot win against a God whose intention is love*'? If so, how does that change your outlook when difficult situations come into your life such as a painful diagnosis, financial difficulty, relationship breakdown or roadblock of impossibility?

- If the richest soil, producing the most abundant foliage, is found in the lowlands, would you prefer to be in the lowlands or the highlands? Why?

- How comfortable are you communing with the Holy Spirit? Has that changed or grown over the years, one way or another?

- Take some time to pray together if you are in a group, encouraging each other and believing for the soil of your lives to be enriched as you move forward in the journey. If you are not with a friend right now, then let me be that friend! *Father, I lift up my friend to you right now, asking that you give them a sense of your presence with them where they are. I pray for the soil of their hearts to become rich with life as they continue in your word and through this book. Bless them now I pray. Amen.*

Part Two

Seed

5

Hope Is Planted

May the God of hope fill you with all joy and peace as you trust in him, so that you may overflow with hope by the power of the Holy Spirit.

Rom. 15:13

Into the Deep

'There are no sharks this time of year,' he said.

It was July 1992 and I was in Melbourne, Australia, on my first missions trip. We were having a day off, learning to surf in the ocean, and I was part of the second group of surfers (I use that term loosely) to enter the waters. Since seeing the film *Jaws* I have refused to enter salt water any deeper than my ankles . . . and even that gets my heart racing. But having been reassured this was not shark season, I walked confidently into the waters carrying my board, hearing surfer songs in my head and dreaming of catching that perfect wave. I was up to my waist in salt water when the instructor – whose side I refused to leave – loudly yelled 'Shark!'

'Very funny,' I said, casting a sideways glance at him.

But his eyes were deadly serious, pointing towards the area where our first group had been swimming. Ominously slicing through the water was a fin, clearly seeking an American-style breakfast. I have never moved so fast in my entire life. In fact, I am pretty sure I walked on water.

Ever since that time, in a literal sense, I have stayed in the shallow waters. Metaphorically . . . I am embracing the deep.

Shallow Living

There is a popular song which talks about stepping into an unknown ocean, trusting God's hand to guide us; it is definitely one of my favourites. And my favourite part is where it mentions trusting without borders – what a stunning image. Shallow living keeps borders within arm's reach; only deep water requires perfect trust. Yet how much of our spiritual lives are lived in deep waters?

Proverbs 3:5–6 ESV is one of my life verses, and one I often put in books when I sign them, because of the depth of its truth: 'Trust in the LORD with all your heart, and do not lean on your own understanding. In all your ways acknowledge him, and he will make straight your paths.'

He will make straight your paths. It doesn't say 'he might', 'he'll think about it', 'he'll wait to see if you've earned it' or . . . It says 'he will'. Do you trust him with this? Can you walk forward not knowing the next step, but trusting that he sees the end from the beginning clearly in this season of your life? Shallow living trusts in our own ability and leans on our own understanding. It acknowledges our own achievements and it looks to guide our own lives. In fact, the world would say we are irresponsible for not being proactive and forging our own way, making logical decisions and ensuring the way forward benefits our own desires. But God doesn't work that way. Who would have known being rejected from Torah school and living as a local fisherman would qualify some young guns to become major players in spreading the gospel around the globe?

Perhaps your life story is not one of prestige, wealth, opportunity or popularity. Maybe you took a few detours on your journey, making unwise choices which opened the door to unwanted consequences. The world would say you are uneducated, it's too late, or you don't look the part. Those qualifications have never come into God's economy. This was true even of Jesus. Isaiah 53:2 says: 'He had no beauty or majesty to attract us to him, nothing in his appearance that we should desire him.' In other words, Jesus was not the coolest person on the planet in terms of looks or popularity, yet that had no negative impact on his purpose being fulfilled.

We should never use our past as an excuse for our present. The Bible does not give us that option in Christ. The apostle Paul says in 2 Corinthians 5:17: 'Therefore, if anyone is in Christ, the new creation has come: the old has gone, the new is here!' If the old is gone, then let it go. Stop sending out search parties to bring it back again, using it to explain behaviour un-becoming to one in Christ. I say this from experience. For years I battled insecurity and fear, knowing that it stemmed from experiences I had had as a young child. It ruled my life for too many years, and even now I must be intentional in not letting fear get a grip on my day-to-day living. To live in fear is to plant myself in shallow waters, ignoring the ocean of promise surrounding me.

As shallow living robs us of deep understanding, so planting a seed of faith in shallow ground will never produce a rich crop. Remember: to go higher, we must go deeper.

Joy and Peace

But to go deeper, we must trust greater.

I find it interesting that Romans 15:13 appears to speak of a God of hope planting joy and peace, in order to reap a harvest of hope. Surely he would plant hope if he was hoping to harvest hope? But if we look closer at the verse we see that joy and peace were not planted – they were grown, in proportion to the growth of trust. You see, God will not automatically plant hope, trust and right decisions in our hearts . . . we must choose them for ourselves. Harvesting a good future always begins with planting a strong trust. If we spend our lives waiting on God to regularly download joy and peace, we will be sadly disappointed. He has already given it in seed-form through the fruit of the Spirit; it is now our responsibility to cultivate what we have been given.

I have learned that joy and peace often grow in the darkest of seasons, not the brightest. Perhaps you've heard the phrase 'dark night of the soul'? I had one of those seasons in my twenties. It was one of the loneliest and most difficult periods I've ever walked through, yet it was there that I came to know the Lord at a level of intimacy I had previously only toyed with. He suddenly became my everything, at a time when I felt I had lost everything – job, income, church, friends, reputation. In my barrenness, I found his faithfulness.

Some years later I experienced something similar. In a season of tremendous lack and loss, I was honestly filled with more joy and peace than I had ever known; in fact, joy and peace were the overarching traits in my life towards the end of that season. Only in Christ can the seeds of suffering produce a harvest of joy. I have preached it many times: there is a side of God we can only meet when we are in deep pain – and it is one of his most beautiful sides.

In Part One I mentioned that we would let God 'dig in our dirt' . . . Take a deep breath, make a cup of tea and relax . . . as this is where it really begins.

I Don't Care

With a deep heart of compassion I ask: will you trust God with your deepest pain? Will you get honest enough to tell him exactly how you feel, not masking it with Christian niceties? I'm not talking about blaspheming God or speaking out of turn; I mean to be honest with him, because he knows it all already. Where have you felt let down? Believed that he wasn't there for you? That he could have stopped what happened and he didn't? These are the types of unanswered questions which can poison our hearts from the purity of trust and surrender.

This isn't a book to delve deeply into answers for unanswerable questions, but let me share one thing I have learned on my journey: leaving the shores of doubt only happened after I received revelation on the goodness of God.

> Leaving the shores of doubt only happened after I received revelation on the goodness of God.

It was the summer of 2009 and life looked very different from what I imagined it would be at that age. I was coming up to my fortieth birthday, realizing all the dreams in life which had not yet transpired: I was not married, did not have children, and was not thriving in ministry the way I had planned. My heart had recently been severely wounded and I seriously contemplated leaving England and returning to the safety of America. Before making that drastic step I flew to Florida, where I was able to stay in a friend's flat next to the ocean for a few days – just me and Jesus. (Though, in all honesty, I had no desire to talk to him at that moment.)

One evening I found myself listening to the waves, drinking a glass of wine and contemplating how life can turn out vastly different from what we have always dreamed. Without thinking, I muttered (whined), 'I just want to get all my ducks in a row' (a phrase which means to get everything in order).

I heard the Father whisper, 'Can I have those ducks?'

'*No*,' was my emphatic answer, said with a metaphorical pout.

'Why not?' I sensed him asking with a smile.

'Because my "big duck" might be your "little duck" and your "little duck" might be my "big duck" . . . I don't want you messing with my ducks.' I said this in an accusatory tone that suggested he had not done very well so far – why give him any further leeway?

'I'll never leave you and never forsake you,' he said.

I flatly replied: 'I don't care.'

I had been in ministry for fourteen years, a Christian for twenty-one years; I had preached the gospel around the world and given my life to follow God's call overseas, but in that moment it all seemed a big waste of time. *If this is what following him brings, then he can have it.* I was done. It is difficult to explain what happened next, except to say it felt as if he took on the role of my parent and without words said, 'How about you go to your room and think about that' . . . and a curtain was drawn between us. He did not leave; he gave me space to think. It was not too long after, when I was taking tentative steps towards him once again, that I felt him say I could ask for three things and he would give them to me. It was like a 'Solomon moment' in 2 Chronicles 1:7 when God said Solomon could have whatever he asked for. I do not know how to explain it, but in that moment I knew a husband and children were not my answer – rather, it was greater knowledge of his character.

I said, 'Lord, I want to know your goodness; I want to know your trustworthiness; and I want you to hold my future in your hands from this day forward . . . I choose to let it go.'

And that was when I saw it. I had been trying to release my future to him, but I was not sure he was trustworthy; and I did not know he was trustworthy because I was not sure he was good. If I could know, and believe, his true character, I could release my future into his goodness. We must get that honest with God.

Give him access to the darkest places of your heart, the rooms which have 'Do Not Enter' written over the doorway. It is at the threshold of those rooms where he asks us to decide: is he good?

To Trust Or Not to Trust

Genuine trust is not shallow; it must have depth – both naturally and spiritually. If we want to trust God at a new level, we must allow him freedom in greater measure. There must be no areas off limits to him. When I'm teaching on this subject I often encourage people to get very honest with him. Tell him your greatest struggles right now, whether they be emotional, sexual, mental or physical; he can handle it. If you are struggling with any type of temptations or sin then talk to him while you are in the middle of the struggle. Invite him in to that place, and allow the Holy Spirit to show you a way out by the power of the word and the purity of his presence. It may happen overnight or it may be a journey you take with him for a season; either way, allow him to be part of your breakthrough story.

Shame has no place in freedom and only in the light can we break what tries to destroy us in the dark. To know how our Father responds to shame we only need to watch his Son. The first part of Hebrews 1:3 says: 'The Son is the radiance of God's glory and the exact representation of his being, sustaining all things by his powerful

Shame has no place in freedom and only in the light can we break what tries to destroy us in the dark.

word.' He is the exact representation of God's glory and being; in other words, discover the Father's nature by studying Jesus.

There are too many examples to list them all, but here are a few of my favourites. In Luke 7 we see Jesus being anointed by a 'sinful woman', that is, a prostitute. Jesus is at the home of a Pharisee, which was an unusual event in itself, when this precious woman steps front and centre, uninvited, and begins anointing his feet with oil, crying and drying his feet with her undone hair at the same time. In those days it was unlawful to even speak to a rabbi in public, let alone kiss, touch, and caress his feet. Jesus remained unmoved in action, but greatly moved in heart.

As the Pharisee formed irreverent opinions of her, Jesus rebuked his lack of hospitality while intentionally praising her act of honour. There was no shame allowed in Jesus' presence, only acceptance and love. We see the same love in the following chapter where a woman who had been subject to bleeding for twelve years sought to touch the hem of Jesus' garment, knowing there was the healing she desired. Again, in that culture, it was unacceptable for a woman on her period to walk freely in public, and if she needed to be out she had to walk around yelling 'Unclean!' to warn off others from drawing near to her. Which means that this precious woman had not felt touch in twelve years. But equally as painful, she had been shamed and rejected by society for those same twelve years. It was a lonely, painful existence. After touching his garment and receiving her healing she had hoped to scurry away, with Jesus and others being none the wiser about what she had done. No such luck around Jesus! He quickly called out for the person who had been healed to reveal themselves, and she came trembling at his feet, knowing she could be stoned to death for what she had done. Instead of condemnation, he gave confirmation: 'Daughter, your faith has healed you. Go in peace and be freed from your suffering' (Mark 5:34).

Peace. Hope. Love. It always has been, and always will be, God's nature when it comes to those seeking repentance and healing. Living in the deep takes courage.

> Living in the deep takes courage.

Jesus can empathize with you – his depth of trust equalled his height of promise. And it will be the same for us.

Father, I pray for my friends reading these words right now. You know the trials they have faced and the journeys they have walked to get to this point. And you see the desire of their hearts to go deeper with you. I pray right now for a supernatural exchange: shame and condemnation replaced with joy and peace. Allow hope to begin rising in their hearts again. Take their hands and gently walk them onto the waters of the deep, calmly assuring them of your love, your care and your attention to every detail of their lives. And in all things, we will choose to give you thanks and praise. Amen.

For reflection

- *'To live in fear is to plant myself in shallow waters.'* Would you say this describes your life? And if so, in what way?

- Are there any rooms in your heart you have kept away from the Lord? What is your greatest fear about allowing him into that space?

- God is good/God is trustworthy/I can release my future into his hands – which one of these thoughts is most challenging for you, and why? What scriptures can you find to support the truths of these statements, and help you move from fear to faith?

- Ephesians 5:26 talks about Christ cleansing his church by the water of the Word. We see in 1 Peter 2:2 that the word is described as milk, and in Hebrews 5:11–14 as solid food; the Bible not only cleanses, but it also feeds. Would you say you need more cleansing or feeding right now in life?

6

The Danger of Assumption

*Wait for the LORD; be strong and take heart and
wait for the LORD.*

Ps. 27:14

Arnold

Every family has them.

Family stories which are told repeatedly, even though you
have all heard them a hundred times before, remembering an
incident which bonded you together . . . or, more likely, which
is highly embarrassing for one particular member of the family.
One such story in our family would be the trip to Michigan's
Upper Peninsula. This was camping-on-steroids – where you
hike to the cabin carrying everything that you need on your
back, as there is no running water, toilet, showers or anything
else remotely resembling civilization on your arrival. Think
what would sound fun to a trained mountaineer, and you will
have an idea of what appeals to my father.

My sister and I were pre-teens and this was as far from my
idea of fun as could be, but I was part of the family and had
no choice, so up went the backpack and out went the modern

comforts for a week. After what felt like endless hours of torture, we had hiked the five miles into the woods and reached our cabin.

While the views were stunning, bathing in a lake of freezing water soon made me too numb to notice. The trip looked like a potential disaster for me and I was counting the days until I could sleep in my own bed again. The only thing I could imagine making this trip any better, as a nearly 13-year-old girl, was to run into a handsome boy stuck on the same island as me.

And that is when I met Arnold.

He was on the small side, very energetic, incredibly persistent and not at all what I expected. From the logbook in the cabin we learned that some others before us had also met him, though they gave him another name starting with an 'A' . . . which would be inappropriate to record here.

Did I mention, Arnold was a chipmunk?

Yep, a rodent.

He wasn't your average rodent (not that I have been acquainted with many, to be fair) – he had a personality. Arnold would literally arrive outside our front door every morning, waking us up singing (I use that term loosely) for his food, which he stockpiled in his adorable little cheeks until you thought they would explode. And then he would run and deposit the bounty in his larder, returning for additional supplies in a few minutes' time. He would hang around us while we sat around the fire, he climbed up my arm and into my hands and he even ate food strategically placed atop my head. Arnold had no fear, and he and I formed a very special bond. He wasn't taking me to the prom, but he would do while stuck out in nowhere land.

Often life hands us a platter of something very different to what we ordered and if we are not careful, we could miss the blessing we've been served. Expectation can be dangerous. One of the most dangerous forms of expectation is assumption, because assumption can blind us to an upgrade.

This Is Taking Too Long

One of my favourite stories in the Bible is found in John 11 where Jesus raises Lazarus from the dead. This particular sibling group of Mary, Martha and Lazarus was a particularly fond one to Jesus; they were some of his closest friends. He had spent time at their house eating, chatting and, I'm sure, laughing together – there was a definite bond. Which makes it all the more unusual that when told of Lazarus' severe illness, Jesus decided to stay where he was for two more days, instead of returning to heal him.

I can only imagine what assumptions must have gone through Lazarus' mind during those two days, if he was even coherent enough to think straight. Possibly he doubted their relationship, thinking it was more one-sided than he had realized, or he may have battled anger at the knowledge that the one who could heal him clearly had chosen not to. I am sure some of us have been there before, thinking, *You could have, God, so why didn't you?*

Jesus clearly said that he only did what his Father told him to do, and said what his Father told him to say, so we know he was not acting out of wilful disobedience or laziness; on the contrary, he was operating fully in the will of God by . . . waiting.

Waiting has never been my strong point. I am that girl in the supermarket who, upon approaching the checkout, is counting the items in people's trolleys[1] and calculating which person looks the most likely to take queuing[2] seriously. I want someone alert, wallet out, poised to pay. We've no time for vouchers[3] people.

No, waiting has not come easy to me. But I can say that I am learning (dare I say, have learned?) that waiting on the Lord carries with it something of beauty not found in other seasons. When I am waiting on the promises of God in my life, I remember that he is a good God, so whatever he chooses for me – in the end – will be good. The difficulty comes in the gap between believing and receiving. For Lazarus (and his sisters) it was between death and resurrection. To the waiting world it looked as if Jesus had completely missed it, made his first mistake, stepped out of character and misplaced his priorities. I am certain we can all relate to the feeling of being forgotten by heaven. And the choice we make in that waiting season has a direct impact on our next season. We will look at this more closely in chapter twelve, but I can say with all honesty that the waiting seasons have become some of my absolute favourites with God. They are excruciatingly difficult, but amazingly beautiful.

And they carry with them lessons we cannot learn any other way; not only lessons, but truths which we will carry throughout the rest of our lives. For Lazarus and his sisters the truth was this: in the timing of the Lord, waiting produced an upgrade. And God is no respecter of persons; what he did for Lazarus, he can do for you.

Do Not Fear

If we aren't careful, assumption can also open the door to fear. As we grow impatient waiting on God, we can begin assuming things of him which are far from the truth, and it is in moments like that when fear comes knocking. There isn't space to go in-depth on the topic, but I would be remiss not to include fear in a chapter speaking about assumption, because fear often (always?) is the instigator of wrong decisions and aborted destinies. Scripture tells us:

> God hath not given us the spirit of fear; but of power, and of love, and of a sound mind.
>
> 2 Tim. 1:7 KJV

> So we have come to know and to believe the love that God has for us. God is love, and whoever abides in love abides in God, and God abides in him . . . There is no fear in love, but perfect love casts out fear. For fear has to do with punishment, and whoever fears has not been perfected in love.
>
> 1 John 4:16, 18 ESV

In these verses we clearly see that fear is not from God; they are powerful verses to memorize and meditate upon if we struggle with fear and anxiety. Regardless of our circumstances, this is truth. Life might be throwing facts at us faster than darts towards a dartboard, but the word of God gives us Scripture to stand on and declare into any situation, believing for faith to overcome fear every time. In the world today fear has become rampant, to the point of epidemic. It is impossible to look at the news, read social media or be in discussions about world events without fear seeping into the conversation. If you doubt this, begin listening to your own words and those of people around you – fear is everywhere. We say things such as: 'I hope I don't catch that [disease]';

'I'm afraid of what the economy will do'; 'I always get ill this time of year'; 'I'm probably going to lose my job'; 'At this rate we'll be broke before we know it'; 'I'm afraid that's just the way it is'; 'I'm afraid my kids will get into that when they're older' . . . and on it goes.

None of those are biblical statements or words of faith. And yet we have become so accustomed to saying them, and hearing them, that anything different sounds out of place. In the last six months I have become extremely intentional in this area and have been shocked at how much fear and negativity I had been speaking in and over my life. I honestly had no idea it was so profuse! Yet, as I have made intentional decisions to stop saying sentences full of doubt and fear, have reduced how much news I read or watch on my phone and have de-friended those on my social media feeds who are extremely negative, I have begun seeing a major shift in my own faith, belief, outlook and sense of peace. It is no surprise – the environment we choose directly affects the healthiness of our lives; so I have decided negativity will no longer be the norm in my world.

> I have decided negativity will no longer be the norm in my world.

I realize that for some this may be difficult as a negative person may be close to you, and you cannot separate yourselves from them. It is not easy to be in that place. I would encourage you to guard your own heart from becoming bitter or prideful and, instead, intentionally come in the opposite spirit. Do not agree with what you do not agree with, but find another way of responding in love, kindness and grace. We are not here to change other people; we can only change ourselves, and that is a challenge in itself!

Out of Control

It will come as no surprise that my previously mentioned frustration at waiting in queues is directly related to my need for control. I am your typical type 'A' personality in many ways. Recently I was preaching and said that a perfect Saturday morning for me is waking by 6 a.m., going for a long run, having my devotions, doing a few loads of laundry, cleaning the house, making breakfast and having coffee . . . all before 9 a.m.

I pretty much lost my audience at that point.

In my defence, although I like to control my environment and am highly self-disciplined, I am much more flexible when it comes to leading other people or waiting on God. I might have some great suggestions for how I think he should work something out, but at the end of the day I trust he is the Creator of the universe and I am . . . Jen. He wins.

Earlier we talked about living as a victim of our circumstances and how that does not reflect trust in the Lord; if that is one end of the spectrum, then assuming we must control our circumstances is surely the other – and neither choice fully trusts the Lord. The times when we feel God is not working fast enough are the times when we like to take the reins, believing that some action is better than no action. And there is, of course, truth in the statement that 'God can't move a parked car' – we need to be doing something in order for him to direct us somewhere. I am not advocating sitting around doing nothing until you have an angel visitation or writing appears on the nearest wall, not at all. As I said, I am a doer and I enjoy doing . . . but I have learned the art of being, and it has changed my life.

Speaking of taking the reins, I remember many years ago when I was home for a visit from university and decided to go riding on my dad's horse. This was not your typical riding horse; it was a Percheron – a French breed. These lovely animals were originally bred as war horses, now used as draft horses or seen in shows. As my grandparents were living on my parents' property at the time, my father bought a few for my grandfather to use in his retiring years. The memory of my grandfather standing behind the horse ploughing the field still chokes me up today; it was beautiful to watch him relive his childhood memories.

But in my mind a horse is for riding, so I asked my dad if I could take Sally through the woods. Dad looked at me as though I had lost my mind, reminding me that these horses were enormous, too large for saddles, and were meant to work, not ride. Ignoring the facts, I persisted. Eventually persuaded, Dad brought a stepladder for me to climb onto the horse's back (told you they were large) and I grabbed hold of the reins and the mane as we gently sauntered towards the woods. My parents have 100 acres of property, so there was plenty of space to walk/ride and I enjoyed thundering down the small hills atop her back, holding on with my legs for dear life – literally!

As we came out of the woods I paused Sally to catch her breath, and mine. She suddenly became agitated so I glanced backwards, just in time to see an enormous horsefly resting on her backside near the tail. As I turned to brush it away, the fly clearly took a large bite out of her bottom because we went from 0 to 60 faster than a Ferrari. I've never been so terrified in all my life (except for the shark incident of course). I didn't have time to readjust myself, so I held on awkwardly with every ounce of strength left in my legs, while I grabbed a handful of the horse's mane and screamed as loud as I could for my father to help me. The horse ran towards the barn, but the speed at which we were approaching meant she had no intention of stopping and saw the road as the better option. Looking frantically to my father for help brought no relief as all I could see was him laughing – uproariously. Gee, thanks, Dad.

Once Sally finally stopped, I jumped off as quickly as I could, hobbled back to my father and angrily asked him why he hadn't done anything? He replied, 'Jen, what would you like me to have done? The horse weighs over 2,000 pounds and was running at full speed!'

Fair point.

Loss of control is scary when we do not trust the one in control. Which returns us to our earlier discussion – is God trustworthy? Until we can answer that with an unequivocal 'yes' we will attempt to take back the reins of control, perhaps missing some of the greatest adventures of our lives. Because, when all was said and done, feeling fully alive atop a war horse was an exhilaration I will never forget. As soon as it was done, I wanted to do it again.

> Loss of control is scary when we do not trust the one in control.

Abraham's Assumption

Waiting for a promise to unfold can increase our fear the longer we wait, tempting us to choose options originally off limits. This is clearly seen in Abraham and Sarah's life, whose assumption opened the door to an act of compromise which continues to impact the world today.

In summary, Abraham was given a promise to be the ancestor of a great nation; at that time he was 75 years old and fertility seemed a lost dream. But he believed God and obeyed what was in front of him at the time, which was a call to leave his homeland for the land God would show him. After eleven years he and his wife were tired of waiting and Sarah assumed the promise could come through Hagar, her Egyptian servant. Abraham readily agreed to this disobedience and Ishmael was born. God clearly said that Ishmael would be a 'wild donkey' of a man with everyone's hand against him . . . and he is the father of the Arab nations we know today, which are continually at war. Assumption is dangerous, on so many levels.

Seeds of promise must be planted deep within the ground of trust, but even there we must guard against the disease of assumption which rises from fear, control and impatience. Is there any area where you are staking your promise on assumption instead of trust? Controlling instead of waiting?

I would encourage you to read Proverbs 3:5–6 again, meditating on the truthfulness of God's faithfulness. Meditate on the ways he has been faithful in your life up to this point, asking him to help develop you in the area of trusting him, more than trusting your circumstances. For it is in the ground of trust that our promised seed begins to germinate.

For reflection

- What have you learned through seasons of waiting on the Lord?

- How much negativity would you say is in your world and comes out of your mouth? Is it easier for you to be negative or positive? Would you say most of the people around you speak negativity or life?

- Would you say that you swing towards the 'victim' or 'controller' side of the spectrum? What changes might you make to help you come towards a centre of peace instead?

- You were encouraged to look at Proverbs 3:5–6 at the end of the chapter – read that in a few different versions of the Bible (*The Message* would be a good choice) and see what the Lord says to you through that exercise – what leaps out at you as you read?

7

The Power of a Promise

And I will put enmity Between you and the woman, And between your seed and her seed; He shall bruise you on the head, And you shall bruise him on the heel.

Gen. 3:15 NASB

The Spotlight

It was a moment I'll never forget.

Before I continue, it is important to mention that while growing up (and until my late thirties) I battled intense insecurity and fear – I mean, intense. Hiding behind my mother, refusing to hold eye contact, face turning bright red when anyone spoke to me, terrified to speak in class and always believing that I was being laughed at behind my back. I lived in a continual state of shame, fear and anxiety. It improved slightly after I became a Christian, but in reality I learned to cope with it, work around it or – most often – put a mask over it.

Despite my debilitating insecurity, I loved the stage. When I stepped onto a platform I came alive, because I could be anyone except Jen Baker – which was the greatest desire of my heart for the first twenty-five years of my life. This particular evening we were rehearsing our high-school play *The Mousetrap*, in which I had the lead female role. It was late, the school had closed hours before, and nearly everyone except the janitor had left the building. I had stayed behind to practise some lines, and that is when it happened.

The director stepped out of the auditorium, and I was preparing to leave when I glanced up to see a small circular spotlight at centre stage. It was just wide enough for one person to be seen. I couldn't pass up the opportunity. Looking around to make sure nobody else was watching, I put my things down and rushed to the platform. I carefully, methodically, made my way to the centre of that light where I stood – just me, the spotlight and my imagined audience.

Time stood still. I wasn't yet a Christian, but I felt something divine over that moment, to the point where I literally could not move. I looked out to the 'audience', took command of the atmosphere . . . and I decided right then and there: this was my destiny.

The seed took root.

The Greatest Seed

I have intentionally spent the first several chapters of the book looking at soil before speaking of the seed, because of the vital role environment plays in growth. But now I want to begin looking at what is planted in the soil we have created. As we have just seen, one of the seeds in my life was that call to be on a platform – from that moment forward I never doubted what I knew to be my future. And within each of us lie seeds of promise and dreams yet to be fulfilled; but as powerful as those seeds are, let us first consider one which is far more powerful, the greatest seed of all: Jesus Christ.

Hebrews 4:15 says: 'For we do not have a high priest who is unable to feel sympathy for our weaknesses, but we have one who has been tempted in every way, just as we are – yet he did not sin.'

Jesus understands. He is the greatest promise ever given to a sin-stained world, yet even though God said it would happen, the miracle did not come to pass easily or overnight. Anyone who has been a Christian longer than fifteen seconds knows that the timing of God is not the same as our timing and his ways are surely beyond our ways. He is impossible to figure out, yet completely possible to know; therein lies a beautiful kingdom paradox.

We often think of Jesus as a baby or a man, but rarely do we contemplate his life before birth – in unity with the Father and the Spirit before creation. John 17:24 ESV says: 'Father, I desire that they also, whom you have given me, may be with me where I am, to see my glory that you have given me because *you loved me before the foundation of the world.*'[1]

And a few verses before that we read: 'And now, Father, glorify me in your own presence with the glory that *I had with you before the world existed*' (John 17:5 ESV).[2]

Even earlier, in John 1:1–3, 14 ESV, Scripture says:

In the beginning was the Word, and the Word was with God, and the Word was God. *He was in the beginning with God*. All things were made through him, and *without him was not any thing made that was made* . . . And the *Word became flesh* and dwelt among us, and we have seen his glory, glory as of the only Son from the Father, full of grace and truth.[3]

> Jesus existed, within the Trinity, before he existed. *That* is the power of a seed.

Jesus existed, within the Trinity, before he existed. *That* is the power of a seed.

It's In There

In school I was never a fan of biology. In fact, anything that remotely resembled the scientific was automatically labelled boring and I would go back to daydreaming. But there was always one activity that would distract me from 'la-la land' – using the microscope. Through its lenses you see visual proof of what you would have otherwise sworn did not exist. That was when I not only learned, but saw first-hand, the microscopic beings surrounding and indwelling (gross) our lives at all times. It was as if this whole other world existed which I had been oblivious to, and I found it fascinating!

Seeds are like that. They contain much more than what the eye can see; as we know, from an acorn grows an oak tree. It is the same with a promise – within a promise lies your future. The promise is simply the beginning, the starting blocks, let's say, but the future is the race you run, outworking that particular promise. Equally, a seed that has perished could be a forest unseen, and a promise ignored might be a blessing unmet or a future not fulfilled. I understand that not all seeds are meant to produce trees, but I believe that all promises of God are there to produce life. Otherwise what a cruel God he would be, promising something he never meant to fulfil. Just as a seed becoming a forest is dependent on a multitude of factors, so are the promises of God – with faith one of the most determining components. The Bible says: 'And without faith it is impossible to please God, because anyone who comes to him must believe that he exists and that he rewards those who earnestly seek him' (Heb. 11:6).

Faith is your key to breakthrough.

In 2 Corinthians 5:7 ESV the apostle Paul says that 'we walk by faith, not by sight'. Even our day-to-day walking, living and believing must be by faith and not by what we see. In other words, we must continually choose to see the forest within the seed, by not allowing circumstances to distract us from God's word and his nature, two keys to creating an atmosphere for living a strong, faith-filled life.

Word and Nature

I do not believe it is possible to walk in the fullness of all that God has promised, without shaping our atmosphere by meditating on the Scriptures daily – yes, daily. The reason I say this is because we live in a world saturated with unbelief, fear and anger. It is filling our eyes and ears at a rate never experienced in the history of the world, through television, social media, smartphones and other forms of media. If we are not intentional in guarding our eyes, ears, minds and hearts then we will unintentionally be affected by the atmosphere around us. Think of it like this: unless protected, we cannot enter water without getting wet.

I am not saying we should separate ourselves from the world; we are in it, and meant to be. But too many Christians are trying to fit in so much, they no longer stand out. We go from one extreme to the other – highly judgmental or excessively accepting. Christ did not judge the unbeliever, but neither did he condone their sin; he invited them to another way. Only by studying the word of God, which is called our sword, can we safely know the leading of God in our lives. We would never enter a battle without a sword, and we are in a daily battle, so why leave it on our shelf at home in the morning? And while having it on our smartphones is good, there is something special about holding the actual pages of the Bible in our hands, highlighting verses and jotting down notes. Call me 'old school', but I believe it makes a difference!

If you struggle to read, as I know we all do at times, then ask the Holy Spirit to help you, and start small. We don't gorge babies with roast dinners and neither should we attempt to gorge on the word out of guilt. Take a small bite; meditate on that small bite; ask God to reveal himself to you through it; worship him; wait on him; and believe it is feeding you, even if you don't feel particularly full. (I will share about this in greater detail in chapter sixteen, giving you several tips to help.)

Atmosphere affects everything. We cannot escape our atmosphere, because wherever we are, there it is – and thank God for that. Like the nature of God, it affects our everyday lives. The nature of God is love (1 John 4:8), or another way we could say it would be the atmosphere of God is love; wherever he is, love is. To try and remove love would be akin to removing earth's atmosphere – it would kill us. Without the love of God, earth would not exist, but due to the love of God it remains. And just as atmosphere affects the growth of plants, so his love affects our growth as believers. As we know his love more intimately, we mature in his plans more fully.

Don't Be Fooled by Sight

When God created, he visualized what did not yet exist; when Jesus died it was also for those who had not yet been created; and when we believe his promises, they *are*, even while they remain unseen. Sight must never – ever – be a factor in believing, especially when it comes to seeds of promise. Smith Wigglesworth said:

> God can work mightily when you persist in believing Him in spite of discouragements from the human standpoint . . . I am not moved by what I see. I am moved only by what I believe.

I know this – no man looks at appearances if he believes. No man considers how he feels if he believes. The man who believes God has it.[4]

> I am not moved
> by what I see.
> I am moved
> only by what
> I believe.

Belief in the unseen creates movement in the seen – because belief in the unseen requires faith and, as we have seen, faith is what pleases God. He desires us to ask him, in faith, for promises he has given us. And, as seen in the following scripture, faith is what moves mountains out of our way:

'Have faith in God,' Jesus answered. Truly I tell you, if anyone says to this mountain, 'Go, throw yourself into the sea,' and does not doubt in their heart but believes that what they say will happen, it will be done for them. Therefore I tell you, whatever you ask for in prayer, believe that you have received it, and it will be yours.

Mark 11:22–24

There are promises I am still believing for, thirty years on, and I will continue believing for them until either I see them come to pass or the Lord directs otherwise. Because I know that God is 'not a man that he should lie' (see Num. 23:19; Heb. 6:18), and though some promises may not come to pass due to factors outside God's control (e.g. our free will), I will continue believing that God gives good gifts to his children, because anything else would open the door to unbelief and doubt, which never produce the peace and clarity of God.

As James 1:6–8 ESV says:

But let him ask in faith, with no doubting, for the one who doubts is like a wave of the sea that is driven and tossed by the wind. For that person must not suppose that he will receive anything from the Lord; he is a double-minded man, unstable in all his ways.

In the last chapter we saw how Ishmael was born to Abraham in a moment of fear and assumption, but in Genesis 21:1–3 we see the promise of Isaac born to Abraham after a twenty-five-year wait:

> Now the LORD was gracious to Sarah as he had said, and the LORD did for Sarah what he had promised. Sarah became pregnant and bore a son to Abraham in his old age, at the very time God had promised him. Abraham gave the name Isaac to the son Sarah bore him.

God does not forget a promise. And Isaac was the first of a multitude of sons born to Abraham, physically and then, through the seed of Christ's sacrifice, ingrafted spiritually – just as was promised in Genesis 17:6–7.

Within the promises you are believing for lie the greatness of God's blessing, goodness and inexplicable creativity to bring about a future beyond what you could dream or imagine. It's all in there. Don't give up. Because this promise is not only for you.

> Within the promises you are believing for lie the greatness of God's blessing, goodness and inexplicable creativity to bring about a future beyond what you could dream or imagine.

Therein lies the true power of a promise – multiplication. Just as an acorn grows an oak tree which produces many acorns, and as Christ brought forth a bride, so our fulfilled promises are meant to bring forth an impact beyond our borders.

For reflection

- Do you tend to struggle more with reading the Bible or knowing his nature? Take some time to chat to God about this and think whether there is a reason you are more comfortable in one area over another. What is one small change you could make in this area? Perhaps it's praying for three minutes a day or reading the Bible for three minutes a day – it's fine to start small!

- *'Jesus existed before he existed'* . . . what does that thought make you feel about your own life? Is it encouraging? Daunting? Hard to comprehend? Or freeing?

- What do you do to intentionally set your atmosphere as a place of faith, in which your promise can grow?

- Take some time to meditate on and discuss what it must have felt like for Abraham and Sarah to hold Isaac for the first time – seeing twenty-five years of waiting, finally come to fruition. How does this encourage you to wait for your own unanswered prayers?

8

The Merging of the Miraculous

And as for you, brothers and sisters, never tire of
doing what is good.

2 Thess. 3:13

Bragging Rights

I'd like to take a few minutes to brag about my mother.

She is one of earth's unsung heroes. You will probably never meet her, she will never be on television and few people outside her own circle of friends and family will ever know her awesomeness. But when I think of perseverance and unremitting belief, she is the first person that comes to mind.

Her spiritual journey really took shape at the tender age of 13, when she felt God might be leading her to become a nun in the Catholic Church. Though the thought was daunting, her greatest desire was to please him; so after plenty of persuasion her parents finally gave their blessing, and off she went alone to continue her education and deepen her spiritual walk with God. It was in the convent where she grew nearer to him, watering seeds of promise planted deep in the soil of her little heart – seeds which had been nurtured by watching the spiritual lives of her mother and maternal grandmother. By graduation, at 16 years old, she felt God say that she had learned what he wanted her to learn, and that he was not asking her to join the convent for life. (I must admit I am quite glad about this, otherwise I wouldn't be here!)

She dated various men, but only once she met my father did she know he was the man for her. Their love story is beautiful, though unfortunately space doesn't permit me to go into detail. But suffice to say they married and she dreamed of happily-ever-after. Just a few months ago we celebrated their fiftieth wedding anniversary, which was one of the most beautiful occasions I've ever been part of. I was so blessed to be home for the occasion, asking them copious questions about the day and their courtship; I will forever cherish those memories.

But as in any relationship which traverses fifty years, there were some challenging mountains to face along the way. One of them was the fact that my mother loved the Catholic Church so deeply, she was certain my father would choose to join and she dreamed of sharing that journey with him. She admits her naivety now, but being young and in love can veil us from even amber flags of warning. Though my father definitely loved God, he did not want to attend a Catholic church, being raised Methodist, and so began many years of them seeing church and God through different lenses. Thankfully God is bigger than a denomination, and their strong love united, rather than separated, them in an issue that has previously divided strong families, let alone strong nations.

My first book *Untangled* was dedicated to my mom, explaining that one of my most cherished memories while growing up was to come downstairs every morning and see her doing her devotions.[1] The picture is etched in my memory and though I did not have much faith until university, her actions silently spoke volumes to me. I would not be who I am spiritually without her influence; and for that I will be eternally grateful. I often tell people she is my rock. And though Jesus is my ultimate rock, her life will always be the first one I think of when seeking to walk more closely with the Lord. She had no idea how much I was watching her when I was growing up. And the fact she never gave up, continued serving God, regardless of the times we may have misunderstood her, and continues even now praying daily for her family, is to me a promise fulfilled from the heart of a young bride dreaming of her future family. It was not easy, but I am grateful.

May each of us learn from my beautiful mother and continue to believe, even in the darkest of times, that God hears our prayers and will answer our cries in his way, if we refuse to give up in despair or give in to doubt. I know two other mothers who understood this principle well, expressing it beautifully with grace and boldness.

Expecting a Miracle

Seeds carry miracles and miracles require outside assistance.

Elizabeth and Mary were the ones chosen to carry that which carried the transformation of humanity. Elizabeth carrying John the Baptist, forerunner to Jesus. And Mary, mother of our Lord and Saviour, Jesus Christ. Two women with vastly different experiences, yet their lives beautifully intertwined by promise fulfilled. In Elizabeth we see a woman older in years, who had suffered deep disappointment through barrenness, yet chose to remain faithful to the Lord, even through the pain of delay and the death of her dreams. We see this description of Elizabeth and her husband Zechariah in Luke 1:6: 'Both of them were righteous in the sight of God, observing all the Lord's commands and decrees blamelessly.'

The couple served the Lord faithfully, though the shame of not having children was immense in that culture. *Easton's Bible Dictionary* says: 'For a woman to be barren was accounted a severe punishment among the Jews' (Gen. 16:2; 30:1–23; 1 Sam. 1:6, 27; Isa. 47:9; 49:21; Luke 1:25).[2] *The International Standard Bible Encyclopedia* elaborates:

> In Israel and among oriental peoples generally barrenness was a woman's and a family's greatest misfortune. The highest sanctions of religion and patriotism blessed the fruitful woman, because children were necessary for the perpetuation of the tribe and its religion. It is significant that the mothers of the Hebrew race, Sarah, Rebekah and Rachel, were by nature sterile, and therefore God's special intervention shows His particular favor to Israel. Fruitfulness was God's special blessing to His people (Exodus 23:26; Deuteronomy 7:14; Psalm 113:9).[3]

Elizabeth served through her grief; she persevered through her disappointment; and she remained steadfast through her unanswered questions. I know it is difficult. Trust me – *I know*. The greatest desire of my heart since I was a child has been to have my own children. From when I was 10 years old and held my recently born brother for the first time, I knew I was created to be a mother. For me, there is no feeling on earth like the joy of holding a newborn, soothing their cries and gently rocking them to sleep. I could spend hours in that position, and have done so, feeling as much at home there as when I am centre stage.

And yet, for reasons I do not understand, I remain 48 years old and childless. I cannot type these words without tears welling up in my eyes and a lump forming in my throat. I have screamed, yelled, cried, begged, pleaded, sworn and wept for hours over the loss of children in my life. At one time I was even close to adoption, only two days from being approved at panel, when a spanner[4] was thrown in the works and it all went to the wayside. I cannot understand the ways of God, and I do not know if I ever will, but please trust me when I say that disappointment and despair have lived alongside my promises for many, many years. I relate to Elizabeth far more than I relate to Mary.

But some of you may see Mary in your mirror. Perhaps you had your future carefully mapped out when an event took place which changed everything. You were thrown off course; plans were tossed out of the window and unexpected change altered your world forever.

Yes, both women carried miracles; but they also carried pain and unanswered questions. We cannot touch the miraculous without addressing the unknown, because miracles are only necessary when all knowledge has been depleted. Choose to believe in spite of fear. Because it was within unanswered questions, an unknown future and personal heartache that the miraculous grew. We must not shy away from pain, but rather embrace a promise – and the Promised One – in the pain. The confusion and hurt may loiter at the side, but it need not hold the spotlight of our story. And I do not know how to explain it, but I can say with integrity that I truly love my life right now. I feel full, blessed, and expectant. The tears are for what has not been; the hope is for what is yet to come.

> We cannot touch the miraculous without addressing the unknown, because miracles are only necessary when all knowledge has been depleted.

If we walk the journey long enough, we will all carry a bit of Elizabeth and Mary in our stories. That is why we need each other; nobody was meant to do this alone.

Save This for Jennifer

A move to London brought to the surface a multitude of fears, not the least where I would live and how I would afford it. I was leaving the safety net of a small seaside fishing town in south-west Devon for the hustle and bustle of the greatest city in the world (in my humble opinion) and, as there was no guaranteed salary at the other end, it would be impossible for me to secure any permanent housing. Soon after I arrived, a woman who was visiting our church asked if I needed a place to stay, as she was renting out her flat for a year while she took work in Brazil. I thanked her but said no, as I didn't have the finances to rent at that time. A few months later I ran into her again, and she repeated the question, and I firmly, but nicely, repeated my answer. To make a long story short, I found myself a month after this conversation urgently needing housing, knowing the money I earned would not get me a cupboard,[5] let alone a bedroom, anywhere decent in the city.

Out of desperation I emailed her and politely asked about the flat. Immediately I received a joy-filled email saying that, yes, it was available and could I view it that weekend? Unbeknown to me the Lord, for several months, had refused to let her rent it to anyone else. She later told me that literally every day God said, 'Save your flat for Jennifer.' Bless her, I was oblivious to this as I continued refusing her offer for months. A lesson learned: don't worry about missing God – he will make sure you get where you need to go, if you are diligently seeking him. I still do not know my anonymous financial donors, but God provided a way when there was no way, and I enjoyed living in beautiful Westminster for the next four years.

Once again, God held my answer before I even knew there was a question. And he does the same for you. You see, before the beginning of time God knew that Mary would be a virgin carrying his Son, Elizabeth would endure nights of weeping and I would need a home. His answer, though unseen for a season, was prepared and waiting for the time when it merged with faith, joined with friends and birthed the miraculous. And I am certain there are other answers patiently resting up his large, divine sleeve for their God-ordained moment in your life!

First, Sow a Seed

But, before the miracle happened, a seed was sown.

Genesis 8:22 says: 'As long as the earth endures, seedtime and harvest, cold and heat, summer and winter, day and night will never cease.'

As long as planet earth exists, the seasons of a seed will remain. And where there is seed – from plants to people – there is life to be reproduced. For example, when God called me from America to England I sold my house, losing a good portion of my pension in the process, yet knowing he was asking me to cut all ties physically so that I would not be tempted to return when it got tough. And as I sowed a house in obedience to him, he has always been amazingly faithful to provide me with housing wherever I serve.

We are familiar with the fact that 'one reaps what one sows' and that you cannot plant apple seeds and expect oranges. It is impossible, unscriptural and not according to God's laws. Each kind produces after itself and that is how it will be for the rest of time. I cannot prove it but I believe Elizabeth sowed generosity in caring for other mothers' children when they needed it. Also I believe that Mary sowed many seeds of kindness and love, which brought her into great favour with God, and so he trusted her to care for his Son, as she had shown care for so many others in her young life.

We reap what we sow. If we want to reap the miraculous through our seed of promise, then we must sow seeds of faith. If we want to share in the miraculous with others, then we must share our seeds of faith. I love the way God allowed Mary and Elizabeth to share this miraculous season together. I can only imagine their conversations, laughter, fears, encouragement and worship as they continued in awe of the destiny on their lives and the miracles in their bellies.

Faith Friends

Who are your 'faith friends'? Isabelle, who graciously (and obediently) saved her flat for me, became a precious part of my story and I will always be grateful to her for this. We enjoyed some beautiful times in the flat, sharing about the Lord and our love for him; and though she is now married and living in America, I still feel connected to her in a very special way. I know my mom has said on numerous occasions that she could not have continued if it weren't for her best friend, Vicki, walking with her along the journey. On those lonely, difficult days it was her friend who prayed with her and encouraged her in the word of God, and Vicki would say my mom did the same for her while raising her own five children.

> Who are your 'faith friends'?

From friendships to flats, we need each other; life is not meant to be lived in isolation. Yes, at times a seed will grow alone, but it never grows isolated from the elements around it. As we saw in chapter seven, even Jesus had the Trinity at the beginning of time – isolation is never kingdom. As we are waiting for promises to be fulfilled, let's be each other's cheerleaders. In a world of competition, crassness and criticism may we emerge distinctively different as brothers and sisters showing love, support and encouragement. Our voices should be the loudest, our networking the strongest and our championing of one another the greatest. Proverbs 27:17 ESV says: 'Iron sharpens iron, and one man sharpens another.'

By sowing friendship with others we will reap friendship at a time we need it most, as seen in Elizabeth and Mary. In the meantime, as you wait, continue trusting that your seed of promise is quietly growing in the background . . . using the silent season to nurture your future promise.

For reflection

- Who are your greatest supporters on the journey of faith right now? Do you feel this needs to change shape and, if so, how?

- Have you ever been misunderstood by those around you as you stood in faith? What has helped you to stand strong amid confusion, hurt or misrepresentation?

- Would you identify more with Elizabeth or with Mary? Why or why not?

- I have talked about sowing a seed to reap a harvest (Gen. 8:22) – in what way have you seen that proven to be true in your own life? Are there seeds of faith you are intentionally sowing right now and if so, what do they look like? (This does not only mean financial seeds – it can be time, encouragement, gifts, etc.)

Part Three

Growth

9

The Purpose of Protection

Now faith is the substance of things hoped for,
the evidence of things not seen.

Heb. 11:1 KJV

What Do You See?

'Jesus, Jesus, Jesus, Jesus . . .'

Those were the only words I could manage to mutter as I stood 15,000 feet above the ground, anxiously perched on the edge of a recently opened plane door, looking wide-eyed through my goggles at nothing but English patchwork fields below. Firmly attached to my back, and rather uncomfortably close, was a male stranger I had met a few hours prior. The wind whipping across my face seemed to mock me as I realized this once-great idea now seemed remarkably stupid.

My biggest problem?

Sight.

I saw what I didn't want to see and I couldn't see what I needed to see.

My view was a wide-open space with no sense of normality or safety. Though I looked for a strong, stable place on which

I could plant my foot outside the aeroplane, obviously I found none. My greatest safety in that moment was found in trusting my instructor and listening to his instructions. We all find ourselves in seasons we want to run away from, but can't, and it is then we need to learn from the novice skydiver: trust your instructor (Jesus) and listen to his instructions. Because what I learned from that terrifying moment was that the smartest thing I could do was actually rest – and by rest I definitely do not mean sleep! I mean rest in the fact that I didn't know how to get myself out of this situation . . . but he did.

Seeing in Silence

Though vision is exciting, it is in the secret place of hiddenness where the real work takes place. It is there that our seed of promise begins to grow when faced with three key areas necessary for future breakthrough: self-reflection, increased hearing and deeper trust.

Let's talk silence for a minute.

As any good professional needs a season of study before hands-on employment, I believe God gives us seasons of solitude before promotion of service. And yet, for many of us, that season of solitude masquerades as a period of punishment. We wonder where God is in this, why he has turned silent and what we have done to 'deserve' it? While there is not space to elaborate on this point, please hear me when I say: God is not causing bad things to happen because he wants to teach you a lesson. That is cruel and he is not cruel; he is love. We have a very real enemy, people have free will, and at times we make poor choices . . . any of which could open the door to pain and hurt. But the love of God for you is never – ever – in question. Regardless of how you arrived at your season of darkness, you are not being sent away to learn a lesson; you are being set apart to prepare for promotion.

> God is not causing bad things to happen because he wants to teach you a lesson.

Embracing that truth releases us to look at our season through another lens; it is like putting on 3D glasses at the cinema and having what was far away and fuzzy become close up and personal. In this fuzzy season of life, we can choose to see through the eyes of heaven, which brings out the colour, vitality and purpose often hidden behind the confusion. It was always there – we simply needed the right glasses.

This reminds me of 2 Kings 6 which describes a time when the king of Aram was at war with Israel, and the prophet Elisha was getting prophetic words to help the Israelites win against him. The king was so incensed that he sent an army to kill Elisha. So, early one morning as the prophet's servant opened the door to get his master a Starbucks (I may have embellished that bit), he saw they were surrounded by an army with horses and chariots. The young man called to Elisha, who stepped up to see the enemy and then gently said, 'Don't be afraid . . . Those who are with us are more than those who are with them' (v. 16).

And then he prayed, 'Open his eyes, LORD, so that he may see.' And the servant 'looked and saw the hills full of horses and chariots of fire all round Elisha' (v. 17).

In other words, put on your glasses.

The enemy might have horses and chariots, but God has horses and chariots of fire. He is always one up on what the enemy holds, because the enemy can only copy – God creates. So, today let's look at our season of silence through the lens of heaven – a lens which sees with the eyes of faith, not the facts of sight.

Repentance and Rest

> This is what the Sovereign LORD, the Holy
> One of Israel, says: 'In repentance and rest is
> your salvation, in quietness and trust is your
> strength, but you would have none of it.'
>
> Isa. 30:15

I remember visiting Israel many years ago and walking through Hezekiah's tunnel (see 2 Kgs 20:20). I've never experienced darkness like it. Once the leader turned off his torch,[1] there was not an ounce of sunlight reaching the centre of that cave; it was the blackest black I had ever experienced.

Sometimes life can feel like that – a season when sight becomes not about what you can see, but trusting what you hope God can see: a way out. Many of us know the famous Jeremiah 29:11 verse,[2] and in this season it probably gets quoted more than any other. And it is true! But we need to remember that God sees not only where we are going, but what is needed for who we are becoming.

Over the last few decades, in the western world, I believe we have been put at a disadvantage by some people teaching a gospel which focuses more on what we can receive than on what we have to give. Too many of us are seeking God for his blessing and neglecting to bless God by our giving. If we have been taught that God exists to make us happy, and all difficulties can be rebuked away, then we are dangerously close to building Christians without a depth of faith to sustain them in the storm. The very place our sin gets highlighted and our faith gets strengthened is often found in the same seasons we have been told are from the enemy and must be stopped. I adamantly reject the idea that God creates painful seasons, but he intentionally uses the attacks of the enemy and seasons of challenge to work all things together for good, including our character development. Although clearly not all the pain we endure is caused by our sin, I have also found that painful seasons soften my heart to the Holy Spirit's gentle voice. I am open to him addressing my sin and shame in a way I may not be receptive to at other times.

I have walked through these deeply dark seasons a few times in my life and each time I have had weeks, if not months, of seeing my sin with new eyes – repenting from a purer heart. I have grieved, not over what was done to me, but what I had done to God. And underneath this cover of grief I have felt his hand of love lift the shame, remove the dirt, embrace my tears and encourage my soul. It is deeply painful, while at the same time beautifully freeing. We must trust that he will never allow us to remain in darkness one second longer than necessary, and that striving to fix things in our own strength will only negate the work he is doing deep within our souls.

James 4:7–8 ESV takes on particular relevance in this season:

> Submit yourselves therefore to God. Resist the devil, and he will flee from you. Draw near to God, and he will draw near to you. Cleanse your hands, you sinners, and purify your hearts, you double-minded.

Maybe now is a good place to stop, reflect and ask the Holy Spirit if there is anything we need to bring before God in an attitude of humility? If we deal with it when protected in darkness, we won't need it addressed when exposed to the light.

Thank you, Holy Spirit, for gently showing us our hearts. We don't go into self-analysis right now, but we do ask you to reveal if there is any area you'd like to chat to us about? We receive your loving prompting and gentle leading. Thank you that your only motive is love. Amen.

Can You Hear Him?

In this season, not only do hearts become more tender, but I have noticed our hearing becomes more sensitive. I encourage you not to be concerned about the length of this hidden season. I know that is much easier to say than to do, but instead put your focus on investing in intimacy and becoming more attuned to God's voice, so that when the quiet season is over you are ready to obey quickly at a new level of attentive obedience. There are many excellent books already written about hearing, but let me remind us of one thing: God wants to speak to us even more than we want to hear; but in his speaking, he may use remarkably few words!

God has never been, and I suspect never will be, one to pontificate. What he says carries impact and each word has meaning. Nowhere in Scripture do you find him rambling on with meaningless chatter. Can you imagine Jesus impatiently looking at his watch, waiting for the Father to stop going on and on about his frustration with the Pharisees . . . definitely not!

No, from what I see in Scripture, Father God is clear, succinct and always – *always* – intentional. So, when he used very few words to perform the greatest act of creation ever seen by declaring 'Let there be light' (or more technically correct: 'Light be'), I believe we should take note.

In the same way, many times Jesus used few words to do his greatest miracles. For example: 'Lazarus, come out' (John 11:43 ESV); 'Go your way; your faith has made you well' (Mark 10:52 ESV); 'Young man, I say to you, arise' (Luke 7:14 ESV) – from these nineteen words he raised the dead twice and healed a blind man.

He used *nineteen* words to raise two dead people and heal one blind man.

Most of us can't pray for our meal in nineteen words!

So, when you are waiting to hear the voice of God, quieten your heart and listen for the still, small voice within. If this is new to you, ask him for one or two words – don't expect to hear an entire sermon. *Your season of hiddenness is a time of growth.* He will put into you what he expects to work through you in your next season. So learn to listen. Ask pastors and spiritual advisers around you for confirmation of what you sense you are hearing, and trust your gut above all things, letting your peace rule all decisions in your life (Col. 3:15). Please trust me on this: you will be very glad, once you are 'above ground', that you spent time bringing your spiritual senses to a new level.

I remember, long before he asked me to move to England, when I was in a season of learning to hear his voice, I sensed the Holy Spirit telling me not to buy the pair of socks I was preparing to purchase. Well, that was just ridiculous! I needed socks, they only cost a few dollars and I had the money to buy them – surely God wasn't bothered about whether or not I buy new socks? But again I heard him say, 'Don't buy them.' In my gut I knew this was an issue greater than socks. So I put them down and walked out, if I'm honest, slightly annoyed at God. In the car I asked him why I couldn't buy the socks and in the quiet of my heart I heard this: *Jen, I need to know I can trust you with the small things, before I know I can trust you with the larger things.*

Moving to England all began . . . with a pair of socks.

The secret place with God is a sacred place for us. It is a place of exploration, questions, answers, and the weaving of relationship cords into an unbreakable bond. And it is here, in this secret season of silence, that we not only learn the Father's voice, but simultaneously discover our own unique sound.

> The secret place with God is a sacred place for us.

Trust without Control

Finally, I believe there is one more important tool we can sharpen while remaining protected in this darkness, and that, again, is trust. After exiting the plane (OK, the instructor had to push me), what commenced was one minute of complete and total free fall. That is sixty seconds, people, and trust me, every one of those seconds felt like a minute! Tumbling, twirling, noise, chaos, everything a blur, earth getting closer, trying not to throw up, 'Please God let the parachute work', rapid descent. It is not at all pleasant.

Until it's over.

But once the instructor decided it was time, the cord was pulled, the chaos stopped, and the most beautiful, peaceful silence I've ever experienced engulfed my mayhem; I found myself floating along the air current of tranquillity, far above every care of the world, amazed at the beauty below me. I realize your silent season may actually sound – and feel – quite chaotic right now.

Trust the instructor.

Because in the darkness God is at work. Just as a seed under the earth is actively growing, so are you – and your promises – in this season. The enemy will do whatever he can to convince you that you've missed it, but he is a liar and the father of lies. It is impossible to outgive God, so whatever the enemy throws at you, the blessings of God will far outreach and overtake even that. There are always jewels to be found in the dark place of the deep. And honestly, all growth is not meant to be seen; in fact, the most important growth always happens in the secret (and often dark) place. God purposefully has us hidden to perform his best work, away from the pull of the world and the judgment of people. These seasons are never wilfully chosen, but they can be intentionally enjoyed.

Because once that parachute opens, you cannot rush the descent.

You just sit back and enjoy the view.

For reflection

- Did you grow up in a house that was comfortable with silence? Are you comfortable with silence? Why or why not?

- I have talked about putting on glasses to see with different lenses (2 Kings 6:17) – read that story again and ask the Holy Spirit what he is showing you through this. If you put on the lenses of heaven today, what would you see differently?

- Difficult seasons can soften our hearts towards repentance. I mentioned taking time to let the Holy Spirit highlight if there are areas of unforgiveness in your own heart, or any other areas you need to confess to him. Don't go searching, but if you know there is an area that hasn't been confessed, would you confess it and receive his forgiveness and freedom now?

- What are some ways you have learned to hear God more clearly? Do you feel that your hearing is clear or is this an area of improvement? Ask him to help you discern his voice more clearly, then enjoy practising hearing from him!

10

The Danger of Doubt

*But when you ask, you must believe and not
doubt, because the one who doubts is like a wave
of the sea, blown and tossed by the wind.*

Jas 1:6

One More Confirmation?

As mentioned earlier, my father is an avid fisherman. There
honestly isn't anything about fishing I think he has yet to learn;
he truly is a master! And when we go fishing together we now
have three rules: Jen doesn't touch the worm; Jen doesn't touch
the fish; and we will attempt to face the sun as often as possible,
for the sole purpose of improving (creating) Jen's tan. Yes, they
mainly benefit me, but spending time with his daughter who
lives overseas outweighs his frustration at me not helping too
much; in fact, I think he secretly enjoys it. Although . . . there
was one day this past summer when I pushed my luck a bit far.

We were out with a friend who had never been fishing, so
Dad was busy helping her learn how to cast, reel in the fish, and
so on. I patiently waited for my hook to obtain bait and then
cast beautifully into the water. Soon I felt a tug on the pole, but

thought it best to wait a moment and make absolutely certain it was a fish before reeling in my winner. After a while, when there was no more movement, I reeled in . . . To my horror the bait was missing. A sly fish had gently nibbled it off while I was waiting for confirmation. With a sigh and a '*Daaad*, I need some more bait, please' I cast once more upon the waters of possibility and waited.

Repeat the above scenario.

About one hundred times.

In an hour.

And you will get a sense of how my father might be feeling about our 'rules'! He repeatedly threatened, with a smile, that I was going to be baiting my own hook pretty soon if I didn't actually catch something. I put on the cutest little daughter smile I could and assured him I was simply fattening the fish up for him to catch another time. Finally I asked what I was doing wrong. He said, 'You're waiting too long. Pull it up the instant you feel a tug.'

'But I want one more confirmation,' I replied.

How many times have we said that to God?

When quite possibly our heavenly Father is on his throne thinking to himself: *I hope they learn to reel in at the first tug of my Spirit . . . because if they wait too long, it may pass them by.*

How Long Will This Last?

We learn this principle from Noah, who obeyed the still, small voice when others, to their peril, wouldn't listen. It is important to remember that Noah was told when his season would start, but not when it would end. I think sometimes we have read the Bible stories so often that we forget the actual men and women in the Bible were seeing and experiencing everything first-hand. They had not yet read the end of the story and had no idea how this particular trial was going to turn out – or, in many cases, if they would even be alive at the end of it. Yet, we sit and read

> If we knew our story's ending, might we live the middle differently?

it in relative peace, because we know the end of the story. If we knew our story's ending, might we live the middle differently? It's in the middle season – the waiting time – when we most often fall by the wayside and take a detour into self-will, personal indulgence or self-pity.

Noah was pretty stuck in his dark season; no detour off this boat was to be had unless he wanted to drown. He had to stay in the – literally – stinky situation in which he found himself. He was surrounded by hundreds of animals, living together on a very large boat, stuck in a flood, for an undetermined amount of time. Every provision they needed had to be with them, as there was no second chance or going back for more – what he saw in front of him was all they had to survive. Imagine how he must have felt, not only to be in the situation, but knowing that the only people with him were his immediate family – having witnessed his *entire* community of friends and neighbours destroyed in one day.

Alone. Despairing. Confused. Uncertain. Afraid. Overwhelmed. Sorrowful.

Stepping out of the accepted norm will always take us beyond the boundaries of our comfort zone.

God had given every person an opportunity to follow Noah, believe his warning and save their lives . . . but none except his own family had listened. I wonder if Noah ever thought to himself: *Could I have done more? If I had said something different would the situation have turned out differently?* I cannot obviously prove this, but I do not believe it would have made any difference at all. Their hearts were hardened to the truth and they missed their opportunity to see that. Opportunity is just that – opportunity. By its very definition it does not have an endless shelf-life. And the truth of the matter is, if we choose to forego our moment, it may well pass us by.

Part of the reason people laughed at Noah was the lack of rain. What they could not see kept them from what they should have seen. They were so focused on what was not there, they refused to contemplate what might be coming. This is a snare that keeps us locked in seasons we were meant to leave long ago – fear of the unknown. They wanted proof of what they had never experienced, before they agreed to make a move. Often we want proof of what the future will look like before we enter into an agreement with it. But that is not faith; that is not even real life. There are no guarantees – except biblical guarantees, because, as I have said previously, God is 'not a man that he should lie' (see Num. 23:19). But once humanity gets involved and free will enters the picture, then God is limited, as he will never force his will on us; we must choose it. And that choice will bring about blessing or cursing, depending on the path it follows – obedience or disobedience. We can trust an unknown future to a known God.[1] The key is knowing *him*, not knowing our future. Because any decision based out of fear is not a good decision, or at the very least, not a wise decision.

Noah had no idea how long this foul season would persist, so after a time he released doves to see if land was nearby. In the same way, we must intentionally seek the peace of God, looking for the land of our next season, because we were not created to live endlessly in limbo. He will bring us safely through soon enough. As the dove brought to Noah an olive branch, symbolizing peace and victory, we also will experience a moment when the Holy Spirit confirms that our time has come to step out of our proverbial boat and into our next season of victory.

Foundational Truths

Although many sermons have purported that Noah was mocked for his big dreams and crazy ambition, there is no biblical proof for this. Yes, common sense would say that people might question an enormous boat being assembled for a flood, when heaven had yet to produce a single raindrop. But we do not know this for certain. So, let's go with what we do know: Noah took a stand against the predictable and did something unusual, unexplainable and unorthodox. Golly, sounds a bit like Jesus to me.

In order to experience the unknown, Noah had to build what others refused to build.

His very life – and that of his family – depended on it. Growth seasons are there for (hang on, this might shock you) growth. Yet, how many of us prefer to navigate growth seasons at breakneck speed? 'I'm happy to grow, Lord, just make it quick!' is our motto. As it would be impossible for life to be sustained outside the womb in the first few weeks after conception, it is also impossible for spiritual growth to occur without the time necessary for maturity. Therefore, I personally am glad God esteems the growth season as necessary *for as long as it takes*. Without this season our future is often aborted and our promises unfulfilled, along with the potential influence God desires us to have for his kingdom. In other words, please do not rush what he has not yet finished. I am sure we have all heard about the importance of laying good foundations when building a house. It is the most boring part of the job, yet the most vital; if the foundation is shaky, the house is in danger.

So, this begs the question: is the foundation you're building today strong enough to hold the future you're believing for tomorrow?

> Is the foundation you're building today strong enough to hold the future you're believing for tomorrow?

Noah's foundation followed the specification of heaven to the letter, and those instructions meant it took one hundred years to finish what was needed for one year of function. In the same way, Jesus waited thirty years to outwork a three-year ministry. Foundation is critically important and the greater the assignment, the stronger the footing must be underneath, and often (not always) the longer the process to develop it will take. So, what is our foundation?

> For no one can lay any foundation other than the one already laid, which is Jesus Christ.
>
> 1 Cor. 3:11

> See, I lay a stone in Zion, a tested stone, a precious cornerstone for a sure foundation; the one who relies on it will never be stricken with panic.
>
> Isa. 28:16

As I shared in the third chapter, it begins with a personal relationship with Jesus; after that, I believe our foundation includes whatever is necessary for us to walk obediently in that particular season. Some will need a greater understanding of Scripture, others might need a breakthrough in knowing the Father's heart, and yet others might need a deeper prayer life to sustain them in the coming season. But only in knowing Jesus, and seeking Jesus, will we know what he wants to build in us during this growth season, as we wait for our fulfilled promise.

Are You Comfortable?

I cannot fathom the smell, sounds or surroundings that Noah's family must have experienced on the ark for that year. To have no running water, lavatory, green pastures, or even a bathtub to escape to . . . for a year! I have new respect for Mrs Noah.

But that is yet another lesson we can learn from the life of Noah and our season of growth – seek peace, not comfort. If we look at the lives of the Bible characters we esteem, and seek to emulate, we cannot find one that lived a comfortable, stress-free, relaxed and always prosperous life. It simply does not exist. Alternatively, we *can* find those who battled giants, lions, armies, self and society to remain true to that which gave them peace. They chose to put the peace of God above the opinions of other people, and that made all the difference in their lives and future purpose. It always has, and it always will.

Jesus in John 14:27 esv says: 'Peace I leave with you; my peace I give to you. Not as the world gives do I give to you. Let not your hearts be troubled, neither let them be afraid.'

What are we allowing to make our hearts afraid in this season? Is there anything stealing our peace in the waiting? If we do not know how to recognize the peace of God then we open ourselves to the lure of the evil one. Because it is in our spirit that the Lord leads us (Col. 3:15) and there the enemy cannot reach us. He can put thoughts in our minds and can throw physical attacks at us, but he cannot touch us spiritually once we are in relationship with Jesus Christ as our Lord and Saviour. From that moment forward we are off limits to him spiritually, unless we open the door and invite him in. So, following peace becomes vital to knowing the will of God. And especially so regarding his promises for our lives.

I remember one particular season years ago where God had given me a promise, and very clearly confirmed it through natural and supernatural means (I'm not giving specific details to maintain the confidentiality of some people), yet that promise never came to fruition, and many people were hurt and confused as a result, not the least being myself. When it all went pear-shaped[2] I was not only devastated personally, but I was embarrassed spiritually. How could I have got it so wrong? In the months following I did hours of soul-searching and even spoke to a counsellor to give me some guidance, as I now doubted my ability to hear God even for small decisions. Her words forever changed my life. After I had shared the situation in great detail with her, she said to me, 'Jen, I can only see one thing you've done wrong here and that is you have not listened to your own gut.'

You see, at the time I had taken on all responsibility for this failure, sure that the issue was me and that I was an embarrassment to God and a frustration to people. But that was a lie the enemy had been using to beat me up and to get my eyes off the truth: in reality, there was some other sin in the camp which I was naive to and God would not bless it while that remained. When she said that I had not listened to my gut, I knew she was right; *something* hadn't felt right at the very beginning of the journey, but I had pushed that aside as nonsense and trusted other voices who were saying the right things, but who could not feel the check in my spirit. The longer I listened to the 'other voices', the quieter the check in my gut became.

It was an excruciatingly difficult lesson to learn, but one I never forgot.

> Peace is utmost in all circumstances.

Peace is utmost in all circumstances. At the end of the day, we are accountable to God for our decisions and our actions. He will not ask me about anyone else, only about my own heart and if I followed him as obediently as I could, not giving anyone else top place. And this is the position we must be in if we want to fully know the will of God and hear the heart of God for our lives.

In one of his essays, well-known English evangelist George Müller listed the following six steps to knowing God's will:

- Seek at the beginning to get your heart into such a state that it has no will of its own in regard to a given matter.
- Do not leave the results to feeling or simple impression.
- Seek the will of God through, or in connection with, the word of God. The Spirit and the word must be combined. If the Holy Spirit guides, he will do it according to the Scriptures and never contrary to them.
- Take into account providential circumstances.
- Ask God in prayer to reveal his will.
- Take all of the above into consideration and then come to a deliberate judgment according to the best of your ability and knowledge. If your mind is then at peace, and continues so after two or three more petitions, then proceed accordingly.[3]

I have used this list numerous times in my life and always found it quite helpful, to keep the main thing the main thing and to protect myself from being led by emotions or the enemy's deception. This does not remove human fear of the unknown, but it brings in God's peace of the known. We must walk by faith in his ability to protect, guide and provide for us far more than our fear of getting it wrong.

Remember, growth in the hidden place is never comfortable, but it is always necessary. As we will see from the seed of Christ planted many years before he would see the light of day.

For reflection

- How would you describe your foundation at the moment? Where might you need to strengthen it in order to carry the future you are seeking?

- How would you feel if you were 'Mrs Noah'? What would have been your greatest struggles spending a year on that boat? And what can you learn from that about your circumstances today?

- Noah had faith to build what others refused to build – would you? Where have you stepped out in faith when others did not agree, or understand, your decision? How did your relationship with the Lord strengthen through that season?

- How have you learned to discern the will of God in your life? Is this easy or difficult for you?

11

The Power of the Prophet

Behold, the virgin shall conceive and bear a son,
and shall call his name Immanuel.

Isa. 7:14 ESV

Experiment or Reality?

'Wouldn't you prefer being deaf to being hearing?' signed a deaf friend of mine one day. Her face fell when I signed back, 'No, I am glad that I'm hearing.'

She asked the question because I was in the midst of an experiment for a university class. Having worked with the deaf for years, and being fluent in American Sign Language, I wanted to identify with their world as much as possible. This led me to visit an audiologist and ask if she could 'make me deaf' for a period of time. Once she recovered from her surprise, she said the best she could do was to make tight ear moulds – blocking out as much sound as possible. 'Let's do it!' I proclaimed with enthusiasm and naivety, and within a few weeks I found myself 'deaf'.

This meant I needed note-takers for my classes, as I clearly could not learn to lipread in the span of a week. I also could not hear on the phone, needing the help of friends to make any necessary phone calls (this was years before smartphones and texting). I remember one important phone call I needed made for me; after my friend finished the call and got off the phone I asked her what had happened. My friend replied, 'Oh, they said it's fine.'

'But you were on the phone for five minutes . . . what else did they say?' I asked.

'Oh, nothing of importance – don't worry about it,' was her reply.

I stood there feeling inept, angry, confused and hurt. This was my phone call, about my life, and yet she treated it as if it was nothing important. As an interpreter I never forgot that moment, and realized then how vastly important it was to give all the information to the client, whether I deemed it important or not – it was their life. To me the experiment was fascinating on so many levels. But at the end of the day, it was an experiment for me, not a reality. And yes, I was happy to receive back the fullness of my senses, knowing that all of them were necessary for me to fulfil what God had purposed for my life.

I Want to Know You

Having the right information is critical to making sound decisions, and in God's economy the smallest detail may be one of the most important. That is why it is crucial to learn the nature of God, and be sensitive to even the most subtle of his movements.

One of my favourite, and often quoted, Bible verses is Ephesians 1:17 where Paul says: 'I keep asking that the God of our

Having the right information is critical to making sound decisions, and in God's economy the smallest detail may be one of the most important.

Lord Jesus Christ, the glorious Father, may give you the Spirit of wisdom and revelation, so that you may know him better.'

Nearly every day I ask God for wisdom and revelation; I want to know his nature, learn his ways and discern his thoughts. Here are a few more examples from Scripture:

> Make me know Your ways, O LORD; Teach me Your paths.
>
> Ps. 25:4 NASB

> Now therefore, I pray You, if I have found favor in Your sight, show me now Your way, that I may know You [progressively become more deeply and intimately acquainted with You, perceiving and recognizing and understanding more strongly and clearly] and that I may find favor in Your sight. And [Lord, do] consider that this nation is Your people.
>
> Exod. 33:13 AMPC

> He made known His ways to Moses, His acts to the sons of Israel.
>
> Ps. 103:7 NASB

Knowing his voice, nature and ways is critical to knowing his will, plans and purposes. We see this in relationships all the time. As we get to know someone, we learn their likes, pet peeves, preferences and personality. This is one of the joys of new relationships, and it is the same with God; he has likes, preferences and personality . . . I am not sure he has pet peeves, though!

God Fingerprints

Having moulds fitted for my ears emphasized for me the importance of hearing. To hear is to gain clarity, understanding and connection. Without hearing someone, it is difficult to grasp nuances of meaning, or emphasis in voice, and to gain a full understanding of what they are trying to communicate. So, how do we hear and know God if we cannot (normally) audibly hear him? I believe it partially comes through the circumstances around us and what I like to call 'God fingerprints'. When someone has spent any time in a room, they leave fingerprints of their presence on the table, cups, computer or anything else they may have touched. I believe God also leaves fingerprints. He touches situations, circumstances and challenges, directing us to where he is working and showing us which way to go. Almost like clues given for us to discover, if we have eyes to see.

If in Part Two Jesus was introduced as the seed planted by the patriarchs, then in this chapter he is the promised seed still 'in the ground'. In other words, a waiting world has yet to see him, and nobody is quite sure what he is going to look like when he arrives. All they know is that the Holy One is coming, but the details up to this point have been a bit vague. Enter the prophetic.

The prophetic has been misunderstood, misused and misinterpreted for generations. Yet I strongly believe in the prophetic gifting and have seen it used too many times to doubt its ability or biblical importance. One website I found has given 353 references of prophetic scriptures fulfilled in Christ.[1] God clearly wanted those who were seeking to know the details around the coming of his Son and our Saviour, yet after an excess of 300 prophecies people still missed it! It is possible to have the fingerprints of God everywhere, and still miss his handiwork. I remember once looking over a stunning English seaside view and saying, 'Aw, Lord, look at that – isn't it beautiful?' And in my spirit I heard him reply, 'I have seen it, Jen . . . I made it!' Fingerprints. I believe his creation is a masterpiece that is often underappreciated. Yet his fingerprints go far beyond the seen. They are found in the random meeting, which takes on significance several years later; or the gentle nudging to turn left instead of right, avoiding an accident on that road; or the child's prayer, which brings the healing. He is always working (John 5:17) on our behalf and the more we expect his fingerprints, the more we will find them.

One of the most significant examples of this in my life was through a denied visa. God had clearly led me to move to England so I put my house up for sale, gave away my possessions and moved countries with literally just a few suitcases holding all my belongings. Though I had researched getting visa approval before coming, I had six months to stay without a visa and I felt God leading me that way – to go and then he would show me the next step. Upon arriving, I phoned the Home Office to ask about staying and they assured me I could apply while in the country, so that is what I did . . . and I was denied. Having left all in America, now being told I had a month to leave Britain placed me in a dilemma, to put it mildly. So, I went to my local MP[2] and asked for his help, which he was not inclined to give. He said, in a roundabout way, that England did not need any more pastors and I should go home. I assured him that God had called me here, I would return, and that I would write him a note once I was back!

On the other side of the Atlantic I faced further challenges, but the Lord prevailed and less than a month later I had returned to the UK, soon putting a note in the post[3] to my local MP. A few weeks later this MP showed up at the church office demanding to know how I had got into the country. I assured him it was God. After that he kept in touch, more out of curiosity than anything else, I think, and would periodically invite me to Parliament, the House of Commons, and so on.

One such invitation, many years later, was to 10 Downing Street, to hear the prime minister speak. It was there I met a lady whom God would use a few months later to strategically alter the direction of my future. If my visa had not been denied I would not have met this MP, and if I had not been at Downing Street I would not have met this woman, and if I had not met her I might not be doing what I am doing

> If we dust off our disasters, in time we may find the fingerprints of God appearing out of the rubble, working to create something beautiful.

today or most probably even writing this book. Fingerprints.

If we dust off our disasters, in time we may find the fingerprints of God appearing out of the rubble, working to create something beautiful.

Spot the Significant

> Therefore the Lord himself will give you a sign. Behold, the virgin shall conceive and bear a son, and shall call his name Immanuel.
>
> Isa. 7:14 ESV

When Isaiah spoke those words it was nearly 700 years before the word came to pass. That is a tremendous amount of time to be 'in the ground' as a promised seed waiting to surface. But the passing of time never negated the fullness of truth.

If God has given a promise then his intention is to fulfil that promise. He would never give a promise which he does not plan on fulfilling, because that would make him a liar, which he is not. The challenge is not knowing when that fulfilment will come about. And it is in that waiting period that most

promises are dug up and destroyed. Imagine digging in the ground to make sure
your seed has started growing – you would
destroy the very process you had begun!
Yet how many of us do that with our own
promise and the desires of our hearts? We
get tired of waiting and decide to help
God along the way, by taking control over
the growth timeline. This aborts the best
plans he has for us, every time.

> He would never give a promise which he does not plan on fulfilling, because that would make him a liar, which he is not.

If we allow, waiting can be a gift.

That is why it's extremely important to record the prophetic
words you have received or the 'God moments' you have enjoyed, writing them down for future encouragement and direction. This includes specific scriptures that God has highlighted
to you (the best way to get prophetic direction is from the word
of God). Especially if you are in a season needing to know an
answer, ask God to show you from his word what his will is.
We must never – ever – make any decision which goes against
the word of God, as that is our basis of truth. With that being said, Scripture must be used as a whole, not picking and
choosing which bits we like for our situations, as the word can
be used to prove just about anything if taken out of context.

When Isaiah gave the above prophecy, God was assuring the
Israelites that he had not forgotten them, the seed was still in
the ground and that he would come forth at the right time
through a circumstance so unusual it would have to be from
God. Because that is normally how God fingerprints work –
they clearly reveal the Father at work through the miraculous
and the microscopic.

In Isaiah chapter 53 we see in more detail the latter part
of Jesus' life, showing the gruesome death which he would

experience before becoming fully alive. Again, the detail given is extraordinary when you think about it, describing 'bearing' griefs and being 'pierced' for our transgressions. Knowing about the cross this makes perfect sense, but for those who had no knowledge of what was to come it would have seemed an unusual description at best. We also see David prophesying about the crucifixion, hundreds of years before that form of execution had even been invented or put to use: 'For dogs encompass me; a company of evildoers encircles me; they have pierced my hands and feet' (Ps. 22:16 ESV).

Once again, through David, the fingerprints of God are seen prophesying a significant future event, while the seed yet remains in the ground.

While we should never super-spiritualize things and attribute to God what might not be his handiwork, equally we must not hold back from giving him glory for all good gifts – small to large – because what we look for, we will find. I regularly thank him for favour in my life, fully expecting to receive favour and blessing everywhere I go. And the more I expect it, the more I find it. And when I do, I smile to heaven, knowing that I've just spotted a God fingerprint over my life.

For reflection

- What are you doing to develop your relationship with God at a deeper level than you knew him last year?

- Where have you seen 'God fingerprints' in your own life? Are you comfortable with the prophetic gifting – why or why not? (When speaking of the prophetic we must always remember 1 Cor. 14:3 which says 'But the one who prophesies speaks to people for their strengthening, encouraging and comfort.')

- Do you believe that *'God is not human, that he should lie'* (Numbers 23:19)? And if so, how does this shape your worldview?

- Spend some time thanking God for his goodness, blessing, provision and abundance in your life today. Worship him for all he has done and all he is going to do in your future – he has declared that he wants to bless us, and he does!

12

Beauty in the Silent Years

*The suffering won't last forever. It won't be long
before this generous God who has great plans for
us in Christ – eternal and glorious plans they
are! – will have you put together and on your feet
for good.*

1 Pet. 5:10 MSG

The Finish Line

I've never birthed a baby, but as mentioned previously, I've run
a marathon.

And I'm convinced there are similarities. Such as wondering
if it will last forever, will your body ever recover, declaring
(screaming) at one point that you cannot go on and verbally
assaulting complete strangers who are only trying to help you.

For me, it happened around mile 21 or 22 (by that time it
is all a blur). Up to this point I had been doing pretty well and
running according to plan, on schedule for a respectable 4 hours
30 minutes finish time. Previous to this I had spoken to an
experienced marathon runner and, desperate for words of

wisdom, I asked for his advice. He said the best advice he could give me would be: whatever you do, do *not* stop running.

I ignored him.

We ran through a tunnel, and there were very few spectators cheering us on, and I was tired, and I was sure the man with all the experience didn't know what he was talking about . . . and did I mention there were no spectators there to see me do it? I walked for about fifteen seconds; that was all it took to ruin the rhythm, break the stride and change the outcome. *A little compromise, unfortunately, goes a long way.*

Once I began running again, I was instantly overcome with the greatest pain I have ever felt in my life. There literally are no words – it was excruciating-on-steroids. Hobbling over to two medics, I immediately became some other woman, yelling at them to help me and shoving aside the one who wasn't doing it fast enough. I was about 5 miles from the finish line and I wasn't about to be held up now – breakthrough was too close. I've discovered this: nearing the finish line is often when it hurts the most.

It is the last attempt of the enemy to throw us off course before we gain traction and run headlong into our next, best, season.

But I am getting ahead of myself. First we must finish our silent season well.

The Land of 'Is'

A few years ago I was struck by the wording of Acts 2:16 KJV: 'But this is that which was spoken by the prophet Joel . . .'

The word 'is' jumped off the page at me – 'this *is* that'. Peter was referring to Joel 2:28–32, which was written hundreds of years before its message came to pass. 'That' was an outpouring of God's Spirit on all people, both men and women. 'This' was the day of Pentecost when a multitude of both men and women began speaking in other tongues and the church was birthed. But in-between were several hundred years of silence, waiting, wondering and hiddenness. It is where we spend more of our lives – between what has been declared and what has been received. Or, another way to say it, between what has been planted and what has been harvested, or . . . between the starting line and finishing line of this particular marathon. It is what we do in that season which greatly affects the level of blessing and impact when 'this' comes to fruition and we receive the long-awaited promise.

How are you enjoying 'is-land'? I think it is ironic that if you put the two parts together you have 'island' . . . because this season can often feel as if we are on a desert island, all alone. It's the season of waiting, transitioning, and growing from seed to sapling. Here God is silent, knowing there is not a tremendous amount to say until the season shifts; we are going through the motions, feeling perhaps a bit bored, wondering if this is all there is for our lives? Our dreams can easily get misplaced and forgotten in this place; out of sight is out of mind – or possibly even out of heart.

But imagine if God had allowed that in regard to the church. What if his Holy Spirit had not been poured out on the day of Pentecost because it had already been hundreds of years of waiting, so why bother now? That is ludicrous to think about and clearly never would have happened. God had a particular promise he had given and he intended to deliver on that promise, at the right time. As we wait for a particular promise to break ground in our lives we have a responsibility to listen, watch, rest and grow in the season to which we have

been planted. To be honest, we had better get used to it, because far more time is
spent in the land of 'is' than in the thrilling
moments of 'this' or 'that'!

> We have a
> responsibility
> to listen, watch,
> rest and grow
> in the season to
> which we have
> been planted.

Even though we spend most of our lives
in this season, it isn't meant to be a season
of sitting on the sofa, waiting for a breakthrough. Waiting involves working, going
after God, gaining strength in the foundational truths and
watching to see where he is working, so that at the right time
we are ready to join him.

Winds of Change

In a well-known speech by former UK prime minister Harold
Macmillan, he said, 'The wind of change is blowing through
this continent. Whether we like it or not, this growth of
national consciousness is a political fact.'[1] It was a controversial
speech, addressed to territories throughout Africa which
were currently under British rule, but whose peoples desired
independence from Great Britain. This led some to praise
while others criticized this political move which would change
the look of a continent forever. Whether you agree or disagree
with the political decision, the prime minister was picking up
on something that I believe is biblical – winds of change.

In the Old Testament we see Moses leading the Israelites
for forty years in search of the Promised Land. As we read in
Exodus 40:34–38, they followed a cloud by day and fire by
night. In fact, verse 37 says: 'but if the cloud did not lift, they
did not set out – until the day it lifted.' They would not move
without movement.

While I wholly agree with the belief that 'God cannot move a parked car', in this day and age I fear many believers take over as their own satnav whenever God seems slow in manoeuvring them from one point to another. *We must not rush what is not ready.* God wants us to know his will more than we do, and he will do whatever he can to ensure that those who seek him (and his will) find it. But he will not do it at the expense of our growth, and if we choose not to seize the opportunity to grow in the dark place, then we may find ourselves circling the same mountain again . . . and again . . . until we do.

When I was younger my sister and I would play hide-and-seek with my father every December, in search of our yearly Christmas tree. Our home had a 14-foot cathedral ceiling in the lounge area, so of course we had to get one that reached the top, much to the chagrin of my mother who had to clean up all the fallen needles! As youngsters, my dad would walk far into the field of trees for sale and with a twinkle in his eye ask, 'Who wants to play some hide-and-seek?' And my sister and I would excitedly say 'We do!' as we immediately closed our eyes and began counting. '1, 2, 3, 4, 5 . . . 10, ready or not, here we come!' we would yell, giggling as we set off, studying the footprints in the snow left behind by my father. I have already mentioned that he could be a mountaineer, so he would cleverly backtrack his own footsteps, letting us, in essence, run in circles. (Parents, this is a great tip for tiring out kids . . . You're welcome.)

I remember one year, when we were cold, tired and frustrated at not being able to find him, and at the point of giving up, we heard a distinctive bird whistle. My sister picked up on it because I was . . . well, quite honestly, I was too busy pouting.

But she heard it, and knew it was the whistle my father had taught us, and our little eyes brightened as we realized – he was nearby! We followed the sound, and found our father.

As an adult, I have since come to learn that my father never once took his eyes off his girls. When he saw us begin to despair, that is when he whistled some direction.

I believe our heavenly Father does the same. We saw this truth in chapter two when God revealed to me burdens I was carrying which were not mine to carry. Remember, he knows when the load is too heavy and the weariness too much. Let's remind ourselves of what he said in Matthew 11:28 (in *The Message*):

> Are you tired? Worn out? Burned out on religion? Come to me. Get away with me and you'll recover your life. I'll show you how to take a real rest. Walk with me and work with me—watch how I do it. Learn the unforced rhythms of grace. I won't lay anything heavy or ill-fitting on you. Keep company with me and you'll learn to live freely and lightly.

Learn the unforced rhythms of grace; in other words, learn to trust the winds of change which release what you need, when you need it. God won't always move us out of the challenging situation quickly, and there are promises we may have to wait a lifetime to receive, but he will always have his eye on us and his heart towards us. Never once will you be out of his eyesight, even for a moment!

> God won't always move us out of the challenging situation quickly . . . but he will always have his eye on us and his heart towards us.

How precious to know that his thoughts to us outnumber the grains of sand (Ps. 139:17–18) and that even at the moment we are reading this, Jesus Christ himself intercedes for us (Rom. 8:34; Heb. 7:25). In this unforced rhythm of grace, I am convinced there is true enjoyment to be had in the waiting room.

The Final Word

I can distinctly remember sitting on my bed one afternoon, realizing that it had been five years since I had seriously dated anyone. I told the Lord that it was *impossible* for me to survive waiting another five years alone . . . Twenty-five years later, and counting, I am still waiting. While I may share more about the journey of singleness in another book, I can say with conviction that there is a contentment in my life right now that I do not believe I could have received through a marriage relationship. Now, I do realize there is also a depth of love to experience with another human which I have yet to experience, so I am not setting out singleness as superior, or saying that I have been called to singleness, because I don't believe that it is or that I have. I am saying there are some promises which take longer than we expect and which carry with them challenges we never thought we would have to face, but a power within the promise never wanes, because the All-Powerful One supplies us with grace for the season.

Let's be honest, we often feel we are the only ones to experience our particular depth of disappointment and despair, but we are not. Everyone – *everyone* – will experience the pain of waiting and promise unfulfilled at one time or another. It is up to us how we choose to respond. Self-pity has never brought about victory, and it never will. Perseverance, faith, hope and trust carry us through seasons we have not asked for, into futures we could not imagine, when put into the hands of a loving Father.

Recently I read a blog by a young woman who was in our youth group many years ago. I was one of her youth pastors and have watched her endure various trials with grace, becoming a beautiful wife and mother to four gorgeous children. Writing about a recent challenge where her sister-in-law faced leukaemia, and graduated to heaven, she writes the following (edited and given with permission):

> *Perseverance, faith, hope and trust carry us through seasons we have not asked for, into futures we could not imagine . . .*

The next morning, when kids weren't able to listen in, I called Donna. She is our administrative assistant at church, and she had just walked through a battle with brain cancer – I remember two things about that conversation that I still carry today.

First, she was filled with compassionate sorrow for our family and for Shannon. Her own journey had made her so very tender to the difficult journey of others. Second, as I sputtered on about it hopefully being treatable, and wanting the doctors to formulate a good plan, she stopped me and said, 'Jennifer, cancer doesn't get the final word; God does.'

God knew I would go back to those words over and over again as I watched my sister battle for her life. When the first round of chemo didn't bring the counts down as we'd hoped, I clung to those words. When she lay in a bed in ICU and the doctors told us we had only hours left, I white-knuckled that truth – God has the final word; not leukemia. When she traveled to Texas for treatment, I continued to believe that God would have the final word. He alone would provide healing . . .

Soon, it will have been 5 months since Jesus called Shannon home. I have made it very clear to our daughters: Leukemia did not win.

Shan did not lose her battle with leukemia. Cancer did not have the final word in her story. The cross always has the final word.

Always.

Because Shannon's story didn't end on March 3 when leukemia took more than what her earthly body could handle – Shannon's story simply took a turn Heavenward.

Sorrow may come in the darkest night, but the cross has the final word.[2]

The winds of change may blow in a direction we do not foresee, but we can always trust the word of God as the final word because his word carries with it hope, and ultimately, life. As Scripture says:

> Now if we died with Christ, we believe that we will also live with him.
>
> Rom. 6:8

> I have been crucified with Christ. It is no longer I who live, but Christ who lives in me. And the life I now live in the flesh I live by faith in the Son of God, who loved me and gave himself for me.
>
> Gal. 2:20 ESV

> For to me, to live is Christ and to die is gain.
>
> Phil. 1:21

Absolutely nowhere in the Bible will you find, *in Christ*, death bringing anything other than overcoming life. His word is *final*. And that final word is what gives us hope that what we are seeing is not all there is, because underneath the ground, in the silent soil, a seed is beginning to change shape and new life is beginning to form – ready to burst forth at just the right time . . .

For reflection

- Acts 2:16 KJV says *'But this is that which was spoken by the prophet Joel'*. I spoke about the word 'is' and living in 'is-land' – in what ways do you feel you are there right now, and what are you doing to enjoy this particular season?

- Do you tend to run ahead of God or to lag behind him? What suggestions would you have for someone who struggles in this area, to trust him more?

- What does the phrase *'unforced rhythms of grace'* mean to you? (Matt. 11:28, MSG).

- How have you learned to trust God in seasons when it seems God has not answered your prayer in the way you wanted him to?

Part Four

Life

13

Breakthrough on the Horizon

I call heaven and earth to witness against you
today, that I have set before you life and death,
blessing and curse. Therefore choose life, that you
and your offspring may live . . .

Deut. 30:19 ESV

The Backstory

Not long ago I read a story on the BBC website about a horse named Metro – who paints.[1]

Yes, you read that right: a horse that paints. Previously he was a champion racehorse, until racing injured his knees and he was, literally, put out to pasture. With a racing career behind him and an uncertain future awaiting him, it did not look good for Metro. He was created to race, so without racing, what future did he have? But one day his new owner noticed that Metro liked to bob his head up and down repeatedly. Being an artist himself, he wondered if a horse could hold a paintbrush in its mouth? Standing next to Metro, he picked a colour and then put the paintbrush in Metro's mouth to see what happened.

Metro began making strokes across the canvas . . . and an artist was born!

His owner, Ron Krajewski, believes painting literally added years to Metro's life. And, on top of that, Metro's paintings have sold well, with half of the earnings given to New Vocations, a charity helping to rehome retired racing horses.

A horse that paints.

I dare believe that Metro will be remembered after he's gone for his painting career far more than his racing career. What we think is the full story of our lives may only be the backstory to what soon can become our best story.

Because that's what promises do: they hold our best story.

Can You See It?

If you've ever planted a seed, there will be that momentous day when, after what may have felt like years, you finally see new life peeking through the ground.

At least this is what I'm told.

Because we know by now that I don't have personal experience with anything that remotely resembles horticulture. But I have seen pictures and read the Scriptures about seeds and they all focus on one outcome – *life*.

'For the earth bringeth forth fruit of herself; first the blade, then the ear, after that the full corn in the ear' (Mark 4:28 kjv).

If we wait long enough, and if the atmospheric conditions are right, then new life will appear where previously only soil was seen. This is when it begins to get exciting! You have waited, believed, prayed, expected and watched . . . and now you *finally* are seeing some movement. In other words, God has not forgotten you, hope is in the air and promise is beginning to peek through the darkness. But do we pull the plant out the moment we see the first signs of a blade popping up? Of course not!

If we remove it too soon, we will miss the fullness of what is being grown.

We must keep believing, until we see the plant ready for harvest . . . that is why perseverance is critical to promise. 'Let us not become weary in doing good, for at the proper time we will reap a harvest if we do not give up' (Gal. 6:9). If we persevere and do not give up, the Bible promises we will reap a harvest. It does not say we *might*; it says we *will*.

Perhaps in your life you are feeling a bit weary of the process. You know the seed of promise has been planted deep in the soil of your faith, where it has remained, waited and grown for an extended period of time; hidden from the watching eye of the world, leaving you to wonder if anything is actually happening. But now, you finally see a bit of green hope poking through the soil of darkness. Could God actually be releasing his intended promise after all these years?

Proverbs 13:12 ESV says: 'Hope deferred makes the heart sick, but a desire fulfilled is a tree of life.' A longing unfulfilled can bring sickness to our heart, if we allow it. That is why we must guard our heart with all diligence (Prov. 4:23), because Scripture alludes to the possibility of it being made sick from disappointment – though it is important to note that it does not deem this a foregone conclusion. Instead, we can hope against hope (Rom. 4:18) until we see what God has for us on the other side of our obedience. We can expect that God is a good God, with good gifts for his children. And believe that the Bible is true, releasing blessing, abundance and prosperity for us as children of God. Finally, we can choose to have faith that the first signs of life over our promises will reap a reward beyond what we can dream or expect.

In summary, let us believe the best and not the worst. I am not dismissing personal pain, deep hurt, unmet expectations or unanswered prayers – not at all; in a broken world those exist and, at times, are

> In summary, let us believe the best and not the worst.

battles we must overcome. But I am saying that lack and pain do not have to be the address where we choose to live. We can move to higher ground, even if that higher ground happens to be found in a valley.

Where Are You Sitting?

Psalm 23 is, I believe, one of the most widely known psalms in the Bible. Two verses jumped out at me recently and I think they fit well at this stage in our journey. In verse 4 the psalmist says: 'I walk through the valley of the shadow of death, I will fear no evil' (ESV) and in verse 5 he says: 'You prepare a table before me in the presence of my enemies' (ESV).

We walk through the valley and we sit down in the presence of our enemies.

How many times have we switched those two, sitting down in the valley while trying to outrun our enemies? The valley is similar to the waiting season we have read about in previous chapters. In this season we cannot see our way forward, we feel shut in, the answers seem miles away and the trek looks too long to endure. That is a valley. And that is where we are meant to keep walking. But there are times in the valley when we can see a table sitting before us. (I'm not sure what's on yours, but mine is overflowing with an assortment of fruit, balanced out by dark chocolate and coffee – the three most essential food groups.)

And it is at that table we can finally stop walking – taking a moment to enjoy the view. To me, a pause has often happened at this stage in the journey – when life begins showing new promise, but perhaps we are still a bit battle-weary and in need of rest. If you notice, the enemy is standing nearby. He has not left; he has only been neutralized by the abundance of God's blessings. I take pleasure in the fact that he has to stand (no chair) and watch me be blessed. I can now begin resting, breathing in the deep beauty of what is in front of me and preparing myself for what is to follow.

> You may be walking through the valley right now, but I assure you there is a table waiting – prepared just for you – with a chair pulled out.

You may be walking through the valley right now, but I assure you there is a table waiting – prepared just for you – with a chair pulled out. Give yourself permission to go and have a rest.

A Promise Is Born

We have looked at natural seeds, but it is by studying the ultimate seed, Jesus Christ, that we find our greatest example of a journeyed promise filled with purpose. Let's recap: the patriarchs planted the seed, the prophets reminded us of the seed to come and now we finally see the seed himself breaking forth into life through the obedience of one amazing young woman, Mary. 'And she brought forth her firstborn son, and wrapped him in swaddling clothes, and laid him in a manger; because there was no room for them in the inn' (Luke 2:7 KJV).

This was the divinely awaited seed looking very different from what many had anticipated – a baby? If the religious leaders had listened to the prophets, they would have recognized this seed as the awaited Messiah. But in their years of slavery the people could only expect what they had envisioned would be the answer – a mighty, powerful king destroying the enemy and releasing freedom. Our promise may look different from what we expect. And if we hold our expectations over its reality, we may diffuse its power. The promised seed born that day was exactly as intended, fully grown to maturity during the years of darkness, breaking forth as . . . a helpless infant. When our promise peeks his head above ground and starts to form before us, we must be careful not to dismiss what might look different from our expectation. Because quite often *what we expect is not what we receive; but what we receive is far greater than what we have expected.* In other words, what looked opposite to the people's expectation opened the doorway to their dreams.

The Lord can do the same in our lives too if we trust him through the process and the pain. Because, as we will see in the next chapter, new birth brings its own set of challenges.

For reflection

- Are there areas of want in your life where you are placing trust in someone or something other than God? Perhaps you are looking to your savings, doctor or spouse for an answer, above God's word and his presence? What frightens you, if anything, about wholly trusting God with this person or situation?

- Have you ever walked in assumption with God – assuming he was going to do one thing, when in fact he did another? What did you learn from that season?

- Where do you struggle most to believe the best and not the worst? Or does that come easy to you?

- If you are walking through a valley right now, I want you to imagine a table laid out for you by the Lord. What would be on it? Picture yourself sitting there with him, enjoying a meal with peace and quiet . . . allow yourself to relax and rest in that picture as long as necessary. See as many details as you can, and revisit as often as you like, he is always waiting for you.

14

The Fragility of new Birth

When the wheat sprouted and formed ears, then the weeds also appeared.

Matt. 13:26

Sounds of the City

I began writing this book a few months ago, looking forward to using my quiet office space where I could literally write for hours at a time, praying over the words, and for those who would hopefully be helped through the pages of the book. So, on that first morning of writing I went for a run, showered, had devotions, made a hot cup of coffee and sat down before my computer ready to create magic.

As described by the Onomatopoeia Dictionary, this is the sound which began literally *moments* after I sat down to begin writing this book: *grrrakka kkakkakkakkakkakkakk akkakkakk kkakka akk.*[1]

That, my friends, would be the sound of a jackhammer – 15 feet from my window.

Out of my mouth came the sigh: 'You have *got* to be kidding', as I rolled my eyes heavenwards for help. Turns out that the house behind me was having four months of building works done, starting that morning. As if that wasn't bad enough, the next day the house outside the other window commenced their own major building works. *Both* sides of my office had major, ongoing, loud, destructive, annoying noise every day from 8 a.m. to 5 p.m. for the next several months.

Birthing something new does not always go according to plan.

The Enemy Is Angry

I do not like giving the enemy much attention; I would much rather talk about Jesus. But we ignore him at our peril. As we learned earlier, he is actively carrying out a strategic agenda in this world: to steal, kill and destroy our lives. And this unfortunately does not stop after the promise begins to take shape. If anything, it intensifies. We see this in the life of Jesus, our promised seed, which broke ground in the last chapter. Most of us know the Christmas story where the wise men visited Jesus in Bethlehem after he was born, having been asked by King Herod to give him an update after their journey, under the guise that he wanted to worship him (Matt. 2:8).

After being warned in a dream not to return to Herod, the wise men left for their home country another way, causing fury in the king once he realized his plan had failed. Meanwhile, Joseph had been warned in a dream to flee to Egypt. I cannot imagine the pressure Joseph must have felt, being the father of Jesus. We often think of Mary as his mother, but Joseph being the father of the house, responsible for the future Saviour of the world, providing for them and ensuring their safety . . . that is no small responsibility!

Thankfully Joseph obeyed and they fled, before one of the most horrific slaughters in history took place: all male children in Bethlehem and the surrounding region under the age of 2 were killed. It was the enemy's first attempt, that we know of, to destroy the seed of salvation after birth. And though it caused unspeakable heartache for many, it failed miserably in its original intent. Because God will protect what God has ordained.

Regardless of what the enemy throws against us, God still has – as we saw a few chapters ago – the final word. If he has ordained a thing, then he plans to see it through to completion. Never has he been taken by surprise or flustered by a complication. He knows the end from the beginning and he is at perfect peace at this very moment. We are the ones who open the door to fear and the enemy when we fail to stay in this perfect peace he has ordained for us. One of my favourite scriptures is found in Isaiah 26:3 NLT: 'You will keep in perfect peace all who trust in you, all whose thoughts are fixed on you!'

> Regardless of what the enemy throws against us, God still has the final word.

Read it again, slowly: 'You will keep in perfect peace all who trust in you, all whose thoughts are fixed on you!'

There is no hesitation, no hedged bets, and no get-out clause – it is the classic 'if . . . then' verse. If we trust him and keep our thoughts fixed on him, then he will keep us in perfect peace. Our responsibility is to listen and obey, to trust and follow what he is saying and where he is leading. Nothing more and nothing less. We may get it wrong at times, but God sees the heart and he knows that if we are honestly seeking him and his ways, then his grace can cover our detours. But if our hearts are not fully trusting, and if we allow fear to gain a foothold in our lives, then we have, in essence, opened the door to another player and limited God's ability to provide his perfect peace.

Where Are Your Weeds?

As mentioned in chapter seven, fear is one of the enemy's greatest weapons, embedding itself in the very fabric of our society through social media, television, music and any other willing outlet. Nearly every news story is fuelled by it, and our day-to-day conversations spread worry and anxiety at a rate equal to wildfire through a drought-filled forest. Fear is one of the most dangerous weeds to affect the garden of our promises. And like most weeds, fear starts small . . . and grows fast.

How many of us have noticed that cultivating beautiful flowers takes a certain level of skill, but growing a weed takes no effort or wisdom whatsoever? Frustrating, isn't it!

Weeds have a life of their own, appearing unwanted and uninvited, walking in with a suitcase like they own the joint. With weeds we must be ruthless, otherwise they will rule us. If we are unmerciful with weeds, why don't we have the same mindset with an enemy out to destroy our lives? I think there are many reasons, but let's look at a few. Firstly, I don't think we understand the power of our words. Look at the following scriptures:

> The tongue has the power of life and death, and those who love it will eat its fruit.
>
> Prov. 18:21

He sent out his word and healed them; he rescued them from the grave.

> Ps. 107:20

By faith we understand that the universe was created by the word of God, so that what is seen was not made out of things that are visible.

> Heb. 11:3 ESV

Words can create, bring healing and produce life or death – they are extremely powerful. If we repeatedly say, and believe, 'I'm poor' or 'I'll never get better', then we can be quite sure that, bar a miracle of God, we will remain in that condition. We cannot continually say one thing and expect God to do another. In his grace there are times he overrides our ignorance, but on the whole I believe he respects our declarations and what we believe, because he has given us free will to act and believe as we like; we are not pawns.

But what if we begin speaking the word of God by saying the following (paraphrased):

I believe God will supply all my needs according to his riches in glory in Christ Jesus.

> Phil. 4:19

Bless the Lord, O my soul, and forget not his benefits, who forgives all my sin and heals all my diseases!

> Ps. 103:2–3

I can do all things through Christ who gives me strength.

> Phil. 4:13

I will trust the Lord with all my heart!

> Prov. 3:5

God will richly provide me with everything to enjoy, so I can do good and be generous in all my ways.

1 Tim. 6:17–18

Then we will begin growing stronger in our spirit and can expect to see the blessing of God in our lives, because we find what we are looking for and see what we seek. For example, have you ever thought about buying a new car, and the moment you start thinking of that make of car you begin to see it everywhere? Why is that? Because you are now seeking what you hadn't seen, therefore seeing what was formerly missed. It is the same with our words. As we speak words of blessing, expectation, goodness and hope, we will begin seeing the fruit of that in our lives and in the lives of our family members. It is a powerful principle: we reap what we sow, and this includes our words.

We can make a decision today to change the words we speak and begin speaking biblical truth rather than worldly facts, such as 'God provides' rather than 'I'm broke'. Because giving expression to anything less than the purity of the word of God and words of life is sowing seeds of weeds,

> Damaging thoughts and life-giving vocabulary will not remain friends for long.

which will not take long to choke the life out of our promises. Remember, words begin in our thoughts. We must be aware of our thoughts if we want victory in what we are saying. *Damaging thoughts and life-giving vocabulary will not remain friends for long.*

Walking in Authority

The second reason I do not believe we get ruthless with the enemy is that we do not fully understand our authority in

Christ. Satan may hold power, but when it comes to our lives, he has no authority. The moment we accepted Jesus Christ as our Lord and Saviour, authority was surrendered to him and the enemy lost – once and for all. But if we return power to the enemy, then we have not used our authority correctly and we have given away ground that is not his to rule. One of the best authors I have read on this subject is Dutch Sheets. In his book *Authority in Prayer* he writes the following:

> Though many dictionaries and lexicons include 'power' in their definitions for authority, strictly speaking, authority and power are not the same. Power is the 'strength or force' needed to rule; authority is the 'right' to do so. They are governmental twins and must operate in tandem; authority without the power to enforce it is meaningless; power exercised without authority – the right to use that power – is usurpation and is morally wrong.[2]

He goes on to say: 'Where God and Satan are concerned, the issue has never been power, including control of the earth. God is all-powerful . . . It is always and only a question of authority.'[3]

We have been delivered from the power of Satan and given authority in Christ to exercise our right to live according to God's principles and the blessing he commands over us through his word. Though it is imperative we *always* walk in this, when we are birthing a new season – believing for breakthrough – I believe our choice of words carries even greater weight. As Jesus' parents had to be aware of the enemy's schemes from the beginning, so must we, the moment our promise starts to appear. We do not stand in fear, nor do we walk in ignorance.

God says: 'I will instruct you and teach you in the way you should go; I will counsel you with my loving eye on you' (Ps. 32:8).

By all means allow the excitement of new birth and a new season to begin to take hold – celebrate what God is doing! Then gird yourself with all the wisdom, strength, knowledge and understanding you have gained in the quiet season, letting your thoughts, words and actions line up with the word of God, as you listen intently for instructions from heaven.

One of the greatest lessons I have learned is this: *God will give, in our hidden seasons, what is needed for our next assignment.* This includes new levels of spiritual authority.

> God will give, in our hidden seasons, what is needed for our next assignment.

If I had the top five lessons of walking with God, that principle would surely be near the top of that list. We must know our season.

Because after receiving our next assignment is not the time to begin studying – all the study should have taken place prior to being given our instructions. Soldiers do not learn to fight after they have been called to combat; they grow strong for battle long before they ever see the battlefield; because if they don't, it will not be long before the enemy takes them out.

For reflection

- The Bible clearly says that God will keep in perfect peace all who trust in him, and whose thoughts are fixed on him (Isaiah 26:3), so would you say you walk in perfect peace right now? If not, what thoughts are keeping you from trusting him?

- What do you do in your daily life to actively come against fear – through the news, neighbours, media, etc?

- *'Damaging thoughts and life-giving vocabulary will not remain friends for long.'* Do you agree with this?

- What does it look like for you to walk in your God-given authority?

15

The Power of Partnership

It's better to have a partner than go it alone.
Share the work, share the wealth.
And if one falls down, the other helps,
But if there's no one to help, tough! . . .
By yourself you're unprotected.
With a friend you can face the worst.
Can you round up a third?
A three-stranded rope isn't easily snapped.

Eccl. 4:9–10,12 MSG

I Need Some Help Here!

It definitely was not the smartest decision I have ever made in my life.

The year was 1991 and I was living in Chicago with a friend, doing our last semester of university with Young Life, working with the inner-city kids of Cabrini Green (a housing estate[1] which no longer exists due to the extreme violence in the area). There are numerous stories I could tell about my time there. Though this one does not involve working among the gangs, it does involve praying for my safety.

I grew up safe and secure in rural southwest Michigan, in the United States. The worst that happened back in 1991 was probably a break-in or theft, but nothing much more sinister than that. It was an idyllic childhood in many ways, enjoying the great outdoors and not fearing to walk down the streets alone. But I was no longer in small-town America – this was Chicago. It was 2 a.m., and my friend Amber and I were walking home after spending the evening watching a film. We joked that possibly this wasn't the wisest thing to do – walk home in downtown Chicago at 2 a.m. – but it wasn't far, and being young meant we were invincible, right?

Walking past an alleyway, we suddenly heard footsteps start behind us. Turning round, we saw a man whose intentions looked less than pure, so we calmly, yet deliberately, picked up our pace. So did he. I took my keys out of my bag, hoping the threat of a stab to the face would deter his intentions. It didn't. There wasn't another person in sight and we had quickened our pace to the point of nearly running when I whispered, with fear and trembling, 'Jesus, we need two angels on either side of us – *now!*'

The minute I said the word 'now', this man suddenly took off running in the other direction – fast! Amber and I looked at each other in shock, said a quick prayer of thanks and basically ran the rest of the way home to safety. I have never forgotten that and have since named my angels 'Bob and Joe' . . . and still call on them whenever I feel a bit nervous. Though I cannot prove they became visible to our potential attacker, I believe they did.

It reminds me of a great truth: no matter how scared we might be, in Christ we are never alone.

Our Unseen Assistance

It is rare to see a plant giving thanks. In fact, if you have seen that, please seek help.

But the fact of the matter is, a plant would not grow, even in the wild, without some assistance, such as the sun, rain and appropriate temperature. Without all three of these, it would struggle to thrive and break through in its next season above ground. Yet, once the rain comes, the sun shines and the temperature cooperates, a plant eventually blossoms out of the ground stronger and more beautiful than the vulnerable seed planted many weeks or months before. But there is still another important ingredient necessary to growth: nutrients. Without seventeen essential nutrients, the plant will not reach maximum maturity and could even show stunted growth.[2] I find it somewhat ironic that one of the main nutrients needed for growth is natural compost and manure. How many of us feel at times that we have been dumped on by a whole pile of . . . poo? Maybe instead of moaning about it, we should see it's there to strengthen the soil in preparation for the breakthrough to our next assignment. (Don't write me nasty letters, please.)

I am being serious. Whatever the enemy throws at us, God wants to, and will if allowed, turn it around for good. We see this all throughout Scripture, not the least – as previously mentioned – in the life of Joseph who was thrown into prison by his brothers at the age of 17. Many years later he was second-in-command of the kingdom and easily could have had them all thrown in prison as payback for his injustice. Instead, he chose to say: 'You intended to harm me, but God intended it for good to accomplish what is now being done, the saving of many lives' (Gen. 50:20).

That is quite an extraordinary statement from one who was wrongly imprisoned for thirteen years. But there was no bitterness in Joseph's heart towards his brothers, only love. Bitterness would have poisoned the promise from breaking forth in strength as it did, but the nutrients of love and forgiveness strengthened the promise while it sat in the muck of despair for those many years. Manure can assist in producing stunning foliage, and forgiveness can help heal even the most damaged friendships.

Let's Talk Forgiveness

The poison of unforgiveness will kill new life faster than a drought in summer. A brief look online shows a plethora of people laying claim to originating the quote: 'Unforgiveness is like drinking poison, then waiting for the other person to die.' Wherever it originated, the truth remains – we cannot hold unforgiveness towards someone and expect no repercussion in our own lives. It will affect us spiritually, mentally, emotionally and, I believe, even physically. I cannot emphasize enough the importance of walking free from bitterness and unforgiveness.

> We cannot hold unforgiveness towards someone and expect no repercussion in our own lives.

The Bible has much to say about this too:

And whenever you stand praying, forgive, if you have anything against anyone, so that your Father also who is in heaven may forgive you your trespasses.

Mark 11:25 ESV

For if you forgive others their trespasses, your heavenly Father will also forgive you, but if you do not forgive others their trespasses, neither will your Father forgive your trespasses.

Matt. 6:14–15 ESV

Be angry and do not sin; do not let the sun go down on your anger, and give no opportunity to the devil.

Eph. 4:26–27 ESV

Be kind to one another, tenderhearted, forgiving one another, as God in Christ forgave you.

Eph. 4:32 ESV

Put on then, as God's chosen ones, holy and beloved, compassionate hearts, kindness, humility, meekness, and patience, bearing with one another and, if one has a complaint against another, forgiving each other; as the Lord has forgiven you, so you also must forgive.

Col. 3:12–13 ESV

Anyone whom you forgive, I also forgive. Indeed, what I have forgiven, if I have forgiven anything, has been for your sake in the presence of Christ, so that we would not be outwitted by Satan; for we are not ignorant of his designs.

2 Cor. 2:10–11 ESV

And forgive us our debts, as we also have forgiven our debtors.

Matt. 6:12 ESV

If anyone says, 'I love God', and hates his brother, he is a liar; for he who does not love his brother whom he has seen cannot love God whom he has not seen.

1 John 4:20 ESV

Then Peter came up and said to him, 'Lord, how often will my brother sin against me, and I forgive him? As many as seven times?' Jesus said to him, 'I do not say to you seven times, but seventy-seven times.'

Matt. 18:21–22 ESV

There are many more I could have included; God is clear in his word – forgive.

I know the pain of this. I have had to forgive a man who molested me as a child. But forgive him I did while driving home one day from one of my counselling sessions dealing with the trauma. Suddenly I was struck with the thought that this man was on his way to hell, and though I felt deep anger towards him, I would not wish any human being to live for an eternity without Christ. And as I prayed for him, I wept – sobbed – begging God for his salvation and to set him free. It was two years later when I finally spoke to him on the telephone and confronted him about the abuse. I will never forget the day he apologized to me, and then uttered these amazing words: 'I became a Christian two years ago.'

'You what?' I asked, not certain I had heard him correctly.

'Two years ago I was driving and I can't explain it, but I suddenly had this overwhelming feeling that I had to get my life right with God. I was driving past a Methodist church, so I quickly pulled in and spoke to the pastor and gave my life to Christ that day.'

I will never be able to prove that it happened at the same moment I was crying out for his salvation, but I believe it did. Because that would be so like God. To take a broken girl's heart-wrenching prayer for her abuser and turn it around for something good.

Blessing and Thankfulness

Forgiveness is not justifying the sin or excusing the behaviour; it is setting ourselves free – free to grow into the fullness of all that God has promised and created us for. It is a decision made, before it is a feeling felt. And sometimes it is a decision, as it says in Matthew 18:21–22, made repeatedly for the same person. I have also had that happen in my own life, needing to forgive many times over. Some of these hurts have been incredibly deep and shockingly painful, and those are the ones most difficult to forgive. At times I have said to God 'I can't do this', because it felt as if I was justifying their wrong actions by forgiving.

In those moments I learned to choose two things: blessing and thankfulness. I would intentionally speak words of blessing over the person(s) and I would maintain a heart of thankfulness towards God, for the many blessings he had already given in my life. I found that blessing and thankfulness eventually broke down the hard wall of un-forgiveness and anger into smaller stones which I used, metaphorically, to climb out of the mountain of pain in which I had been living.

> In those moments I learned to choose two things: blessing and thankfulness.

As I said, many times I needed to bless the person(s) repeatedly, several times a day perhaps. Once I got breakthrough in my own heart, then everything else eventually fell into place and suddenly I would find myself thinking of them without that accompanying knot in my stomach.

A quick prayer will not heal deep wounds, bar a miracle from God. And if this touches a nerve for you, then please spend time in prayer or speaking to someone else to help you get further breakthrough. But if you are wondering how to pray and where to start, I offer the following prayer as an example:

> Father, thank you for loving me and forgiving me when I have needed it. Lord, you know the person(s) who is causing me pain at this moment. I am struggling to forgive them as I've been forgiven, but I choose right now to bless them. I ask that you bless_____ [insert their name here], wherever they are. Please bless their home, their family, their work and the desires of their heart. I choose forgiveness by an act of my will and I thank you for this ability to forgive. I release them from any desire for repercussion on my part. I ask this in Jesus' name and by his precious blood, shed for our freedom and restoration. Amen.

I realize that may have been extremely difficult for you to do. Again, please seek out a friend or a counsellor to speak to if it has brought up any strong feelings or deep wounds, as I would never want you to walk through this alone.

Walk with Me

Part of the reason the enemy tries to destroy relationships is because he knows the power of unity. Genesis 11:1–8 says this:

> Now the whole world had one language and a common speech. As people moved eastward, they found a plain in Shinar and settled there. They said to each other, 'Come, let's make bricks and bake them thoroughly.' They used brick instead of stone, and bitumen for mortar. Then they said, 'Come, let us build ourselves a city, with a tower that reaches to the heavens, so that we may make a name for ourselves; otherwise we will be scattered over the

face of the whole earth.' But the LORD came down to see the city and the tower the people were building. The LORD said, '*If as one people speaking the same language they have begun to do this, then nothing they plan to do will be impossible for them.* Come, let us go down and confuse their language so they will not understand each other.' So the LORD scattered them from there over all the earth, and they stopped building the city.[3]

Here we see what happens negatively if people are in unity, but surely this shows the power of unity for the good as well? The scripture says *nothing would be impossible* for them. I believe that is why the Lord confirmed the promise through a combination of different people from the very beginning: through Elizabeth's pregnancy, the wise men's visit, Simeon's praise song and the elderly Anna's prophetic declaration (which chapter eighteen will look at in more detail). Within a relatively short space of time others were brought around Mary and Joseph to show they were not alone, but instead God was watching out for them closely and deliberately.

I believe it is also part of the reason that one of the first acts of leadership Jesus did after he was commissioned into ministry was to choose twelve disciples, and out of these twelve grew three of his closest companions: Peter, James and John. It's the reason David had Jonathan, Paul had Barnabas, Elisha had a servant and Jesus sent them out 'two by two' (Mark 6:7) – we are not meant to do this journey by ourselves.

Just as a naive girl in Chicago needed an angel and a plant needed some nutrients, we need to maintain unity and relationship at all cost if we want to see our promises and purposes in this life successfully – and powerfully – fulfilled.

For reflection

- Where and how have you seen the 'manure of life' bring blessing into your life?

- Has there ever been anyone you really struggled to forgive? What helped you to eventually make that decision and walk in freedom?

- Who are you struggling with today that could use your words of blessing instead of words of accusation? If you cannot do it to them personally, in prayer would you speak those words of blessing, asking the Lord to bring breakthrough and freedom both for you and for them.

- Where do you see the greatest unity in your life right now and with whom? What is happening as a result of this?

16

Seasonal Upgrade

Then you will know which way to go, since you have never been this way before.

Josh. 3:4

A Great Impact

I've often wondered what pioneering in the early days of America would have been like, forging a new life in an uncharted homeland. I think it might feel somewhat similar to an experience I had years ago with my car. A friend and I were invited to hang out at a lakeside cottage which belonged to the parents of a mutual friend. After buying the chocolate and picking up the films, I was more than ready for a night with the girls. Driving my little red car to the top of the hill, I parked it in the reserved spot behind a railway sleeper.[1] I don't remember much of the evening, as the next morning eclipsed all other memory of that weekend.

My friend had to be at church earlier than us, so she left instructions to lock up and headed off. As we were preparing to leave, the Sunday morning silence was shattered with what can only be described as an enormous collision. I came out

of my room, looking at my friend wide-eyed, who was looking as bewildered as me. Neither of us knew what had happened, and after seeing nothing out of place inside the house
we decided to look outside. I will never forget, for as long as I
live, the next ten seconds. I was standing behind her when she
opened the side door and – to my horror – all I could see from
around her shoulder was a red car . . . sticking out of the neighbour's basement window. Yes – sticking out of the window.
Life immediately felt it was moving in slow motion and I heard
myself scream, 'My dad's going to *kiiilllll mmmeeee*!'

My friend finally mumbled a wimpy 'It's going be OK',
clearly not believing a word she was saying. 'My car . . . is
sticking out of the neighbour's house,' I replied flatly, not in
the mood for platitudes.

We moved closer to peruse the damage and try to surmise
what had happened. To this day I don't know what took place.
We looked up the hill and the tyre tracks showed that the car
had somehow moved over the sleeper to roll down the hill. As
it had lightly snowed the night before, you could see the tracks,
aiming straight for the house, and the bedroom where I had
been standing, when just before impact it suddenly veered to
the left and ran into the neighbour's window instead.

How does this relate to American pioneers, you ask?

The car went where no car had gone before, leaving a path
behind, producing a great impact upon arrival. And isn't that
what we are also meant to do?

Don't Look Back

Sticking with the pioneer theme a minute longer: once the pil-
grims left the shores of England, there was no going back. It was
not like today where you could easily catch the next flight home

if the prospect of uncharted territory was simply too daunting. Perhaps we need to live a bit more like that in our spiritual lives?

I like how Oswald Chambers says it in *My Utmost for His Highest*:

> Every time you venture out in your life of faith, you will find something in your circumstances that, from a commonsense standpoint, will flatly contradict your faith. But common sense is not faith, and faith is not common sense. In fact, they are as different as the natural life and the spiritual. Can you trust Jesus Christ where your common sense cannot trust Him? Can you venture out with courage on the words of Jesus Christ, while the realities of your commonsense life continue to shout, 'It's all a lie'? When you are on the mountaintop, it's easy to say, 'Oh yes, I believe God can do it,' but you have to come down from the mountain to the demon-possessed valley and face the realities that scoff at your Mount-of-Transfiguration belief (see Luke 9:28–42). Every time my theology becomes clear to my own mind, I encounter something that contradicts it. As soon as I say, 'I believe "God shall supply all [my] need,"' the testing of my faith begins (Philippians 4:19). When my strength runs dry and my vision is blinded, will I endure this trial of my faith victoriously or will I turn back in defeat?[2]

Common sense and faith are not compatible.

If we want to grow into the fullness of all that God has planned for us, then we cannot stay in comfort or common sense for too long, because comfort will lie to you and common sense will confuse you. Comfort will tell you that it is too hard and common sense will say it is impossible; neither of which are true through the lens of faith.

> Comfort will tell you that it is too hard and common sense will say it is impossible; neither of which are true through the lens of faith.

Jesus even replied, to someone who made a common-sense suggestion, 'No one who puts a hand to the plough and looks back is fit for service in the kingdom of God' (Luke 9:62). Living the abundant life, believing for the impossible and stepping out of the familiar requires us to look forward, eyes fixed on the prize in front of us, not allowing the regrets of yesterday to steal the expectation of tomorrow. Here is another reason we walk in forgiveness: it cuts off the chain of resentment and bitterness from tethering us to our past season.

Upgrades are always found in our future, never our past.

That is why I love seeing people over the age of 75 still focused on their future, pouring into the younger generation, excited about what God is doing in their lives now and looking towards heaven with great expectation of what is to come. My determination is to live life well and to the fullest, expecting to be healthy, whole and praising God until the moment I step into glory and see my Saviour face to face. I have requested that I be preaching when I step across the threshold – speaking his praises one minute and the next moment beholding him in all his glory. I cannot think of a better way to get my ultimate upgrade!

Because up to that point we are being transformed 'from glory to glory' or – another way to say it – 'from upgrade to upgrade'. It started with the New Testament being a type of upgrade on the Old Testament (Matt. 5:17) and continues with us as believers becoming upgraded from one level of glory to another, into the image of Christ. And just as a plant needs maintaining once it has gone from seed to sapling, we must also maintain our spiritual walk once the promise has begun to show potential.

Start Enjoying the View

After a plant breaks through the soil of restraint, there is a view previously unseen from its days/weeks/months underground. Suddenly there is colour, activity, fresh air and previously unseen possibilities. Now, most plants clearly aren't aware of this and unless you have the imagination of a child it may be hard for you to picture a plant's excitement at bursting through the barrier of earth to the waiting world above. Thankfully, I have a child's imagination. Or I've been writing for too many hours. Because I can vividly picture a wide-eyed sunflower popping through the soil, smiling at the sunshine on his petals, looking to high-five the neighbouring flowery friends sprouting up alongside him. They are all looking around at what, below ground, they did not know existed, just beyond the soil ceiling above them. (You're picturing a smiling sunflower now, aren't you?)

Never let a ceiling stop you from breaking through, because every new breakthrough will bring with it an extraordinary view you never knew existed. And while that may intimidate those of us slightly wary of change, it opens up the possibilities of experiencing a slice of life we have not yet experienced, or even dreamed about. Perhaps God is moving you from the city to the country, or the country to the city, or perhaps into a new job, higher position or long-awaited relationship. Each one brings the joy of promise fulfilled but also the uncertainty of future unseen. If we do not step out, then we cannot step up. And if we do not step up, then we cannot see out, from a higher plane and different vantage point.

> Never let a ceiling stop you from breaking through, because every new breakthrough will bring with it an extraordinary view you never knew existed.

We've Lost Jesus

A different vantage point is exactly what Jesus started bringing to the world around him once he came of age to do so. The first glimpse we see of this is when he was 12 years old, lagging behind from a road trip home. We read about it in Luke 2:41–52:

> Every year Jesus' parents went to Jerusalem for the Festival of the Passover. When he was twelve years old, they went up to the festival, according to the custom. After the festival was over, while his parents were returning home, the boy Jesus stayed behind in Jerusalem, but they were unaware of it. Thinking he was in their company, they travelled on for a day. Then they began looking for him among their relatives and friends. When they did not find him, they went back to Jerusalem to look for him. After three days they found him in the temple courts, sitting among the teachers, listening to them and asking them questions. Everyone who heard him was amazed at his understanding and his answers. When his parents saw him, they were astonished. His mother said to him, 'Son, why have you treated us like this? Your father and I have been anxiously searching for you.'
>
> 'Why were you searching for me?' he asked. 'Didn't you know I had to be in my Father's house?' But they did not understand what he was saying to them.
>
> Then he went down to Nazareth with them and was obedient to them. But his mother treasured all these things in her heart. And Jesus grew in wisdom and stature, and in favour with God and man.

It is a parent's worst nightmare – their child goes missing. I can imagine Mary and Joseph frantically running up and down the stream of Jewish friends and family, asking everyone if they had seen Jesus? Looking at all the children playing, finding his close friends to interrogate, their heart rates increasing with every passing minute. Not only have they lost their child . . . they have lost God's Son. No pressure there, people.

As we see, eventually they realized he was not with the group and so they set off for Jerusalem, where he was last seen. And even there it took *three* days to find him. I think we sometimes skim over that bit because we know the end of the story. But Mary and Joseph did not. Imagine the first day – nothing. The second day – nothing. I can picture them praying, crying out to the Father, seeking forgiveness for their inattentiveness, splitting up to cover more ground, coming back together again, only to be disappointed that neither had Jesus in tow with them. This was long before mobile phones – no texting updates or posting it on social media. But on the third day (where have we heard that before?), hope popped its beautiful face above the parapet of despair. They found him in his Father's house – the place all hope can be found.

Perhaps you need a new perspective on circumstances right now. In this season your promise is beginning to peek over the embankment, beckoning you forward, and as much as you long to follow it, you still face fear of the unknown. What will it look like in a new season, away from the familiar and the routine? Run to your Father's house – his presence. Because it is there you find answers, peace, strength and direction for the journey ahead of you.

And Finally . . .

I love the fact that Jesus needed to grow physically, but also in wisdom, stature and favour. We do not know much of his childhood, but we do know that he, as we do, had seasons of growth, change and maturity before his promise was ultimately fulfilled. And the way it says this came about was through obedience (Luke 2:51). We cannot underestimate the power of obedience to God and his word. In a society which thrives on independence and rights, the kingdom rules with obedience and righteousness. Here are just a few reminders:

> And this is love: that we walk in obedience to his commands. As you have heard from the beginning, his command is that you walk in love.
>
> 2 John 1:6

> He replied, 'Blessed rather are those who hear the word of God and obey it.'
>
> Luke 11:28

> But whoever looks intently into the perfect law that gives freedom and continues in it – not forgetting what they have heard but doing it – they will be blessed in what they do.
>
> Jas 1:25

Blessing follows obedience, every time. If we want to see our promise move from seedling to fully fledged promise fulfilled, then we must walk in obedience to the word of God. That is our guide, our handbook for living and our daily sustenance for faith (Rom. 10:17). Few upgrades will happen without the word of God richly dwelling on the inside of us, feeding us daily.

I mentioned earlier that I would give you a few suggestions to help in this area:

- Start small! There's no rush to read from Genesis to Revelation in a year; if a few verses a day suit you, go for it.
- Use different versions. Choose one easier to read such as *The Message*, The Passion Translation or New Living Translation. (When I became a Christian at the age of 19, I bought a Children's Bible to learn from because the others were too intimidating. Don't compare yourself with anyone else; this is *your* journey.)
- Read a scripture in a few different versions and write down the differences you see, asking the Holy Spirit to highlight lessons to you.
- Always pray before you read, asking the Holy Spirit to help you learn.
- Set an alarm for five minutes and then stop reading at that point; chances are that you will want to continue reading, increasing your desire to go further.
- Start in the gospels (Matthew, Mark, Luke and John) by studying the life of Jesus, asking the Holy Spirit to reveal what you can learn from his life.
- Begin to ask the 'who, what, when, why and how' questions over the passage that you read . . . write down your observations. Then ask yourself: 'How does this apply to my own life?'
- Read the biblical proverb of the day – in other words, if it's the 27th of the month then read Proverbs 27. There are thirty-one proverbs, so you will always have one to read.

- Have a friend read the same passage as you so you can discuss it, perhaps reading a book of the Bible over a week and then meeting for a coffee and chatting about it the following week. Partner up with someone else who struggles in this area (many people do) and cheer each other on.

Obedience brings prosperity and blessing; it's biblical. And as we walk obediently to God and his word we cannot help but prosper in our own lives, through fresh perspective and spiritual upgrade. We must be strong in this area for what our promise brings next – influence.

For reflection

- Aside from missing the obvious benefits we enjoy today, would you have wanted to be a pioneer in the early years of pioneering? In what way does your life currently resemble a pioneer?

- What do you think about the statement: common sense and faith are not compatible? How have you seen this in your own life?

- What does it mean to you to be transformed from 'glory to glory' (2 Cor. 3:18 NKJV).

- Do you find it easy to read the Bible? If not, which suggestions from the book might help you in this area? If you are in a group, share with each other how you study the Bible and what tips have helped you during the 'dry seasons'.

Part Five

Epoch

17

Anointed for Purpose

*So Samuel took the horn of oil and anointed him
in the presence of his brothers, and from that day
on the Spirit of the LORD came powerfully upon
David. Samuel then went to Ramah.*

1 Sam. 16:13

Send

It isn't often that we have a life-changing day.

Mine happened on 28 August 2003.

A month prior, the Lord had interrupted my world with
a vision and mandate to move overseas and now I found
myself staying with near-strangers in the Devonshire countryside, seeking his confirmation for such a big move . . . ideally
through a talking donkey or handwriting on the wall. I needed
something *concrete* because that, of course, is what faith is all
about (said sarcastically).

So, here I was, walking past thatch-roofed houses and gazing
at cows chewing the cud, unfazed by the life-altering decision
looming in the air before me. I hung over the gate, watching

the uninterested animals, when finally I sputtered through salty tears and faltering lips: '*I'm so scared.*'

The cows kept eating.

I felt perfect peace.

And it was then that I knew.

This was a leap of faith . . . I would get nothing more from the Lord until I made a decision. Mustering every ounce of courage I owned, and wiping my tears, I took one last look at the bored bovines, when suddenly an immovable determination washed over me. I marched back to the cottage with my faith stirred and my future focused: I was moving from America to England.

Without speaking to anyone, I quickly walked to my hosts' office, logged in to my email account, cursed the slow internet connection and typed a message telling my boss that I was quitting my job and moving to England as soon as possible . . . Then my finger hovered over the 'send' button for about fifteen seconds.

I knew the moment I hit that button, the trajectory of my life would change forever. I thought of my family, friends, the new home I had recently bought, the indoor decked-in hot tub (I often remind God that I have sown a hot tub), and all the familiarity of southwest Michigan and American culture. In that moment I had little experience, but I had great faith.

Send.

From This Day Forward

David had that type of day when Samuel's horn of anointing oil declared him king of Israel. I imagine he had been doing his normal shepherding duties, avoiding the mocking insults of his brothers, sticking close to his beloved sheep, writing music and practising his trusted slingshot. It was just your normal Tuesday.

Until it wasn't.

Suddenly, he heard his name being called and he was summoned to the house for a meeting. As we read in 1 Kings 16 the rest is history, and that evening he laid his head down – the old smell of sheep mixing with a fresh smell of oil. Life can be like that. One minute it is normal and the next you think to yourself: *How did I get here?*

> Life can be like that. One minute it is normal and the next you think to yourself: *How did I get here?*

Scripture says that from that day on, the Spirit of the Lord came powerfully on David and he was no longer a shepherd boy, but now a king. The problem was: he still looked like a shepherd boy.

Appearance takes a while to catch up with calling.

You may feel ready for your promise to be manifested, but God knows when you are actually ready. (Even Jesus needed to wait thirty years before the seed became the Saviour, so let us not despise our own waiting season.) Though David was anointed king, he still served as shepherd. In fact, not too long after the anointing took place his brothers went to war and David had to stay at home looking after the sheep, longing to see battle himself. After all, this was his kingdom! But instead of ruling he was asked to deliver some bread and cheese to the guys on the front lines. Ignoring the fact that he was just a 'cheese boy', David seized the moment and literally ran towards the battle, longing to be in the thick of it, regardless of how the opportunity presented itself.

The mantle of our calling rarely unfolds in the way we think it should; more often than not, it is unveiled through a side door, not the front door. As he approached the fighting and heard Goliath roaring out his threats, breathing fear over the Israelites in dragon-like fashion, David looked around for the guy stepping up to take down this enemy. And found none. Because this was his battle to win, not as shepherd, but now as king.

Throwing off the armour of another, he lifted up his slingshot and, again, ran towards the enemy. He had killed animals much swifter than this giant could move. David was not concerned about taking Goliath down because he had experience on his side. We know the rest of the story. David gave what I believe to be one of the most impassioned speeches in all of the Bible, found in 1 Samuel 17:45–47 ESV:

> Then David said to the Philistine, 'You come to me with a sword and with a spear and with a javelin, but I come to you in the name of the LORD of hosts, the God of the armies of Israel, whom you have defied. This day the LORD will deliver you into my hand, and I will strike you down and cut off your head. And I will give the dead bodies of the host of the Philistines this day to the birds of the air and to the wild beasts of the earth, that all the earth may know that there is a God in Israel, and that all this assembly may know that the LORD saves not with sword and spear. For the battle is the LORD's, and he will give you into our hand.'

I cannot read that without wanting to jump on a horse and spear something! Notice how many times it says the word 'will' in those few sentences, and how it sounds if we read them with emphasis:

This day the LORD *will* . . .

I *will* strike you down . . .

I *will* give the dead bodies . . .

. . . he *will* give you into our hand.

There was literally *no* doubt in the mind of David who was going to win this battle, this war and this land. He was walking in his new identity even before that identity was widely known.

Even after Goliath fell, David did not reveal his calling; he served another man's vision until the Lord opened the door, at the right time, for his promise to reach fulfilment. And though we don't know David's exact age at the time of being anointed king, scholars estimate he was around 15 years old, meaning he waited another fifteen years to finally walk in his calling (2 Sam. 5:4).

It is important to remember he never – ever – went back to being a shepherd boy.

See the Season

What does our new season look like? Can we describe it in detail? Habakkuk 2:2 says: 'Then the LORD replied: "Write down the revelation and make it plain on tablets so that a herald may run with it."' How will we know if we are in our new season if we do not know what we are looking for?

There are some, I believe unhelpful, teachings out there that claim we should just wait on God to reveal his will, and whatever will be will be. We can pray, but regardless of prayer God will do whatever God wants to do, because he is God, after all. And in principle I understand why that teaching exists and I probably would have adhered to that at one time myself, feeling it wrong to put my will on an all-knowing God. I mean, who am I?

But that is just the point.

Who you are is a child of God, blood-bought, sanctified, redeemed, righteous, carrying the mind of Christ and the Spirit of God, with all of heaven on your side and angels waiting to obey your bidding. That is pretty powerful stuff! God does not want us to remain at the maturity level of a child, and children are often subject to the will of their parents. They cannot drive themselves, or until a certain age even feed or change themselves; they are fully dependent on the decisions of the parent. But in the same way children mature and grow into capable adults, spiritually so should we. We should become capable of thinking and believing what we want to see come to pass, trusting the peace of God on the inside to check us if we step off course. Anything less than full partnership with God in our journey is due either to a lack of trust or simple irresponsibility. And to be honest, not accepting responsibility may also stem from fear.

We saw at the beginning of the book how dangerous fear can be to our promises and it is good to be reminded at this stage as well. Just because we have birthed a promise does not mean that fear takes a bow and exits stage left. It will always look for an opportunity to skew the plans and purposes of our lives, keeping us in the fog of indecision, if we allow it. Having clear vision of purpose helps us prevent that from happening, because if we are familiar with the road, we won't fear the fog.

Taking Hold

Just as a trapeze artist must let go of one trapeze bar to grab hold of the next, so must we. It is impossible to keep one foot on the west side of a river and another on the east – at some point we must decide where we want to stand. One definition of the word 'epoch' in the online Oxford Dictionary explains that it can be the *start* of a period in history or in someone's life.[1] This stage of the journey is exciting; all that has been is poising us for all that will be.

This is not the time to prepare or learn; it is the time to burst forth with new life, seizing the opportunities we had only dreamed of in the not-too-distant past. Here is where David becomes thankful he had never run from a lion or a bear, but instead had used every ounce of courage to do what God asked him to do. The grip on his slingshot and the faith to grab the lion's mane was the same grip and determination he would use taking down the giant. It seems there is often one last push of the enemy before we enter our next season. He tries to throw us off course, make us doubt our decision, or question our ability.

> The grip on his slingshot and the faith to grab the lion's mane was the same grip and determination he would use taking down the giant.

His ways are not new, but they are also not nothing. They can easily throw us off if we get our focus in the wrong place for any amount of time.

I remember sitting at my desk in Grand Rapids, Michigan, struggling to focus because I had only a few weeks left before moving overseas. Here, I had a secure position as a Missions and Community Outreach Pastor, a new house, family, friends and a good income. It had taken many, many years of hard work, but I finally felt secure and on target. Thinking about all of this, I was gripped with fear. Nobody knew me in England; I would have no job, no home, no friends . . . not even my own dishes or bath towel. I sat there in fear, wondering if I could do it. Finally, I picked up the phone and called my friend Amber, sharing my doubts and fears about taking this leap of faith.

She wisely said to me, 'Jen, even if things don't work out in England you can always come back home with your head held high, because you will have tried.'

And that gave me peace.

I could come home.

The door was still open; those closest to me would not reject me for trying.

Her support changed everything that day. I renewed my courage, straightened my shoulders and secured my grip . . . I did not need to know the outcome – I only needed faith to believe for the next step.

The *Sunday Telegraph* reporter Jake Wallis Simons writes this about learning to swing on a trapeze:

> The fact is, getting the hang of the basics of trapeze is easier than it looks. The momentum does a lot of the work for you; and as your arms are locked, it is not overly difficult to maintain your grip. So long as you can commit to the idea of 'flying', as it is known, and jump off the platform like you mean it, everything falls into place.[2]

The momentum works for you . . . it's not overly difficult to maintain your grip . . . so long as you commit . . . jump off the platform like you mean it . . . everything falls into place.

This is what stepping into a new anointing, a new season, looks like. The momentum of all that has gone before us, all the training we've received from the Lord and the character building he has produced in us for the next season, is now ready to propel us towards the place God has designed for our future. Allow your grip on his presence, word and prayer to remain steadfast; then commit and jump like you mean it.

For reflection

- Which moments for you have been 'life-changing'? Were they decisions within your control or out of your control? And how did that make a difference to the impact it had on you, if it did?

- Where do you think the line is drawn between our responsibility and God's responsibility? When should we wait and when should we be proactive?

- Has there ever been a time when things didn't work out and you needed to 'come home', so to speak? How did that make you feel, and who was there to help you process what had happened? Have you ever been the one to help someone else in that situation and how did you help them?

- Take some time to dream. Write out what your promise is going to look like, who it will impact, how you see it playing out and who you would like to bring on the journey with you. It might be leading a Bible study, starting an orphanage, building a business, pastoring a church, paying off your mortgage, getting married, having children or writing that book. Dream!

18

The Danger of Giving Up

Let us not become weary in doing good, for at the proper time we will reap a harvest if we do not give up.

Gal. 6:9

I'm Going to Change the World

I don't know her name. I'm not even sure where we were for this conversation. But I will never forget her face. The year was somewhere in the mid-1970s and I was about 6 years old. To my little eyes she looked about 95 (which means she was probably my age now), with grey curly hair, glasses and a kind face. Leaning down to my level she sweetly asked me what I wanted to be when I grew up.

Looking her squarely in the eye (which was extremely out of character for me) I boldly declared, 'I want to change the world!'

She smiled.

And then she said, 'Ha! Oh, that's sweet. No, really, what would you like to be? Would you like to be a veterinarian like your daddy?'

'I . . . want to change the world,' I said, now a little quieter and a bit more unsure of my answer.

She paused, looking down at me forlornly. Then she said – smiling with her mouth but not her eyes – 'Well, that's nice' . . . and she walked away. Leaving me standing there dejected, alone, confused, and insecurely wondering, *What was wrong with my answer?* I can still feel the rejection and confusion in my heart now, all these years later.

I used to think how sad it was that she had missed an amazing opportunity to encourage a young child in her dreams. 'Of course you can change the world!' 'Anything you want to become, you can become!' These are the words we should speak over young children and she could have said something similar to my little dreamer's heart. But the older I have become, the more I wonder if her reaction was a reflection of her own lost dreams, rather than my bold, childlike ones.

The apostle Paul in 1 Corinthians 13:11 says: 'When I was a child, I talked like a child, I thought like a child, I reasoned like a child. When I became a man, I put the ways of childhood behind me.' Maturity is important for a human and for a believer, but growing beyond childlike faith is never a step towards maturity; it is a turn towards mediocrity . . . which, as it happens, is a close cousin to lukewarmness.

Lukewarm Christianity

Stepping into a new season requires faith and focus. Childlike faith believes, regardless of what it sees; the same way that clear focus remains, regardless of the fog. Yet in order to do this well, one must remain vigilant, aware of the high calling of following the Lord. In Revelation 3:16 the Lord says: 'So, because you are lukewarm – neither hot nor cold – I am about to spit you out of my mouth.' Strong words. Words I never want thought about me, let alone said to me.

The Lord would prefer someone cold towards him rather than apathetic, as would I, to be honest. Have you ever been around someone who is disinterested, lackadaisical or half-hearted? Perhaps a teenager! It is hard to know where someone stands when they are not honest with you and only agree with what you say, never taking a stand or giving an opinion on anything. Or when they grunt one-word answers, not wanting to be fully involved in anything going on around them. Such an attitude can arise from insecurity, but it also shows up in apathy.

At some stage we (should) grow out of this. We realize that life does not operate on our terms and that hard work is necessary for any type of growth or advancement. The Laodicean church did not seem to grasp this, even though they were wealthy and had all their needs taken care of. And this is what I think made Jesus so angry – though they had many material possessions, they were lazy with what they possessed and for this reason the Lord called them 'wretched, pitiful, poor, blind and naked' (Rev. 3:17).

I will never forget an experience I had as an early teen, eavesdropping on the telephone – this was before the days of mobile phones, when you actually had cords and a receiver. Some younger readers may need to google that. Anyway, being a curious child, I would sometimes listen in on phone conversations if the person talking was in another part of the house and did not hear me pick up the additional receiver in a different room. I would not normally stay on for long because I felt guilty or, more realistically, got bored. But one day it all stopped. My father had picked up the phone in another part of the house, and I wondered who he was talking to, so I carefully and quietly picked up another receiver. I did so just at the point where I heard my dad say something like: 'Tammi [my sister] is the one who works really hard. Jennifer isn't a very hard worker – she's a bit lazy.'

I was devastated.

Slowly I replaced the receiver. And I cried.

That was what my dad really thought of me – I was lazy.

The reason this crushed me so much was that I knew what he meant . . . and he was right. When it came to cleaning, helping around the house and earning money for chores, I was not very keen and would often give up before I had finished. I had a creative mind and wanted to be outside, playing, dreaming and imagining myself changing the world and being a princess warrior – everything else paled in comparison to this. Who has time for chores when the world needs rescuing? Looking back, I am glad I had that experience as it made me work harder and it knocked me out of my lackadaisical lethargy, showing me that hard work was important and that it pleased my father.

Now, before you write me a letter, I do *not* believe that we earn anything from our heavenly Father. Our salvation is a free gift given by grace, not by works. God is not asking me to work hard for his love, acceptance or any other gift. At the same time, the Bible is clear that work is important and God honours those who work hard. You only need to read the parable of the talents to see this (Matt. 25:14–30). The apostle Paul even said: 'Those who don't work won't eat' (see 2 Thess. 3:10). Hard work is not a swear word and in a world of 'I want it now', it is becoming even more important to show an example of working with diligence and patience.

Entering a new season takes effort, and once you have persevered through the difficult seasons of darkness, you cannot afford to go on holiday spiritually; if anything, this is a time to press in even more and see God spread your influence further afield.

The Promise

> God never made a promise that was too good
> to be true.
>
> D.L. Moody[1]

I love the above quote because it reminds us of God's omnipotence, generosity and ability. If God has said it, then it is possible – Anna and Simeon are testament to that. In Luke 2 we read how Simeon was righteous and devout, the Holy Spirit was upon him and he was waiting for the Messiah's entrance to Israel. He had been promised that he would not die before seeing the Anointed One (v. 26) and he aimed to see that promise fulfilled because he knew that once he had seen Jesus face to face, there was little the world would hold for him any more. We read in verses 27–28: 'Moved by the Spirit, he went into the temple courts. When the parents brought in the child Jesus to do for him what the custom of the Law required, Simeon took him in his arms and praised God'.

Moved by the Spirit . . .

In other words, he was waiting, listening, ready and alert. Many – many – years had passed, many babies had come and gone through the temple courts and none of them moved him. I wonder if he woke up every day wondering if that was the day. Was he mocked by others for the fact that he refused to give up his dream? Did his family call him crazy and laugh among themselves behind his back? Because that is what dreamers often have to contend with – the mockers. You rarely enter a new season without a few mockers trying to knock you back into last season. Or said another way: those sitting in the crowd of spectators may not fully appreciate those playing on the pitch. It is the perennial seat-warmers who often miss the moving of the Spirit, more concerned with comfort than conflict.

As I am typing this, I sense someone has been moved by the Holy Spirit; you have walked through your waiting season and you know that now God is leading you to step out, but there are voices of doubt ravaging your mind. The naysayers are calling you a dreamer and fear has gripped your heart. Yet in your spirit, the still, small voice is speaking quite clearly. Seek wise counsel, and trust what you hear God saying. Don't give up. Persevere. Believe. Be adamant in your declaration. Keep your eyes fixed firmly on the Lord and follow the moving of the Holy Spirit. Refuse to be paralysed by indecision. God will lead you towards peace and prosperity, and a good future filled with hope and expectation. He will not harm you, but will help hide you under the shadow of his wing. He is trustworthy. His timing is perfect. And his heart is always – always – towards you.

New Season, New Authority

Whether Simeon had prophesied previous to this or not, we don't know. But we know that in this moment he proclaimed and prophesied a difficult word to Mary and Joseph:

> Then Simeon blessed them and said to Mary, his mother: 'This child is destined to cause the falling and rising of many in Israel, and to be a sign that will be spoken against, so that the thoughts of many hearts will be revealed. And a sword will pierce your own soul too.'
>
> Luke 2:34–35

The seed has now become a type of sword, one which even Mary could not avoid.

The seed has now become a type of sword, one which even Mary could not avoid.

Imagine speaking these words to a new, very young, mother. That her child would cause many to fall and would even tear apart her own heart. It was necessary for Simeon to speak these words in order to fulfil prophecy (Isa. 8:14–15), regardless of how difficult it may have been, looking into the sweet eyes of Mary. Though we cannot know for certain, I believe Mary quietly nodded or somehow acknowledged that she knew what he said was truth, for she had already pondered not only Jesus' future, but her own. At a young age she had the spiritual maturity to know that the road ahead was not an easy one and the spiritual authority to say yes to her angelic visitation. And as we read in Part Four, promotion requires us to walk in maturity and authority, because maturity without authority may miss opportunity.

In fact, this is so important that I want to pause and add on a further bit of teaching here. In Matthew 16:19 Jesus says: 'I will give you the keys of the kingdom of heaven; whatever you bind on earth will be bound in heaven, and whatever you loose on earth will be loosed in heaven.' In ancient days the steward to the king would have ownership of the keys and he would control who was allowed to see the king. Often those keys would be worn on his shoulder so that as he walked down the street people could hear the keys banging together, letting everyone know he held access to the king. In the same way, we have been given keys to the kingdom and we have authority, through Jesus Christ, to declare a thing and believe it will happen, if it lines up with the word of God. Whatever is a 'yes' in heaven should be a 'yes' on earth, but we need to say it and believe it.

Dutch Sheets in his book *Intercessory Prayer* writes: 'it is imperative that we remember we are not trying to defeat the devil. He is already defeated . . . Power never was and never will be the issue between God and Satan. Authority was the issue . . . Power does the work, but authority controls the power.'[2]

We have authority through Christ to legislate what happens on earth. There is much more to be said on the subject, but it is not for this book. I would encourage you to read more on this topic if it is new to you; too many Christians are unaware of the authority they carry and therefore, I believe, are not moving in that authority at the level that God would like them to be moving.

Speaking of authority, there is one more bold woman who knew that this little boy was a world-changer, and she was not ashamed to declare it:

> There was also a prophet, Anna, the daughter of Penuel, of the tribe of Asher. She was very old; she had lived with her husband seven years after her marriage, and then was a widow until she was eighty-four. She never left the temple but worshipped night and day, fasting and praying. Coming up to them at that very moment, she gave thanks to God and spoke about the child to all who were looking forward to the redemption of Jerusalem.
>
> Luke 2:36–38

We now see a woman prophesying that this infant is the long-awaited Messiah. Imagine: the majority of her adult life had been spent worshipping, praying and fasting, uncertain as to the reason why, yet in that moment she knew it had all been leading up to this point. She recognized the Messiah, touched him and declared him to all who would listen. I imagine she may have felt as Simeon did – once you've gazed on his glory there is nothing else on earth to hold your attention. We see both a prophet and a prophetess declaring, from the very early days of his life, the authority Jesus carried – before he could even crawl, let alone do miracles. Your purpose was etched in you before you even became aware of it, and as you mature in Christ, your authority should mature with you. 'Your eyes saw my unformed body; all the days ordained for me were written in your book before one of them came to be' (Ps. 139:16).

This new season God is moving you into . . . he has known all along that you are more than able. In fact, he has taken time to fashion you, strengthen your character and prepare you for where he is leading. As happened with Abraham in the Old Testament, and Simeon and Anna in the New Testament, you too may wake one day and find yourself face to face with the long-awaited promise staring back at you. And I believe that if we asked Simeon, Anna or Abraham, they would all say that day was most definitely worth the wait.

> This new season God is moving you into . . . he has known all along that you are more than able.

For reflection

- If God has you in a season of waiting, where things seem to be unfolding differently from how you thought, then ask him what he is wanting you to see and who he wants to be for you. What aspect of his gracious character does he want to extend to you? If you are able, take time to stop and journal those answers.

- Have you ever had someone steal (or try to steal) your dreams? How did you respond? Would you respond differently now?

- We can never underestimate the power of perseverance. Do you find this easy or challenging? Where and when are you most tempted to give up and what do you think the Lord would say to you about that?

- How do you feel about the thought that the enemy is *already* defeated? How do you show in your own life that you believe this statement, or what are some ways that you could show this in the future?

19

The Power of a Purpose

*For I know the thoughts that I think toward you,
saith the LORD, thoughts of peace, and not of
evil, to give you an expected end.*

Jer. 29:11 KJV

An Open Door

Have you ever had a plan 'go south'? The Christmas tree
doesn't look like the one in the magazine; the house build
takes months longer than it should have taken; the great
business idea was better left in the shower; taking two small
toddlers to the supermarket was really as stupid an idea as your
mother told you it would be. Perfect plans which have become
perfect disasters, despite your best efforts.

There was a season in my life when I felt spiritually and
mentally flatlined, exhausted physically and unable to work.
Doctors could not diagnose the cause and I spent weeks
barely able to walk, let alone do much else. It was at a time
in my life when things were starting to move, opportunities

were beginning to emerge and I finally had a vision for my future – which, through this illness, came to a faltering halt. Looking back, I am glad it did, because that allowed me to hear God's still, small voice when he asked me to move countries. Previously I had been running so hard and fast that I'm not sure a megaphone connected to earth from the courts of heaven would have penetrated my focus.

Remember what was said earlier: *what looks like a plan gone wrong may actually be a door pushed open.*

Plan versus Purpose

> Don't confuse the plan with your purpose.
> A plan can be dashed by circumstances,
> timing or lack of resources, but purpose
> cannot. If your dream can be dashed, it is
> because you haven't reached high enough; you
> have mistaken a plan for your purpose.
>
> Stephen DeSilva[1]

Here is where I believe we can confuse matters – by making our plan the purpose, when in reality, it is only the plan. The well-known Bible verse at the beginning of this chapter is often translated to include the word 'plans', but in reality the original Hebrew word means 'thoughts', as you see in the King James Version. God knows what he thinks towards us, what his thoughts are for our future, what his intended purpose is in our lives . . . and it is good. But when we experience a plan going differently from what we expect, our immediate thought is often negative. Remember my visa being denied? I cried buckets of tears when I received the denial letter from the UK government and thought, *How could I have got it so wrong?* I was embarrassed, humiliated, confused and bereft at the news, but what I did not realize was that in the courtroom of heaven, purpose overrides plans.

If God has not locked the door, then do not throw away the key.

There Is a Day

We have seen the promised Christ first mentioned in Genesis, prophesied about in Isaiah, birthed in Luke, and now emerging fully into purpose through his baptism in Matthew:

> Then Jesus came from Galilee to the Jordan to be baptised by John. But John tried to deter him, saying, 'I need to be baptised by you, and do you come to me?'
>
> Jesus replied, 'Let it be so now; it is proper for us to do this to fulfil all righteousness.' Then John consented. As soon as Jesus was baptised, he went up out of the water. At that moment heaven was opened, and he saw the Spirit of God descending like a dove and alighting on him. And a voice from heaven said, 'This is my Son, whom I love; with him I am well pleased.'
>
> Matt. 3:13–17

I remember my own baptism, both of them. Before you get theologically bent out of shape, let me explain. As an infant I was baptized into the Catholic Church, my mom being a Catholic and wanting us to grow up in the church. Obviously I don't remember any of that as a baby, but after making my own decision to follow Christ at the age of 19, I decided that I wanted to be fully immersed in water. So on 22 July 1991 I went into Lake Michigan and was baptized; coming out of the water was one of the greatest moments of my life – I felt an overwhelming joy and peace.

Several years later, while on a tour of Israel, the pastor leading our team announced that anyone who wanted to be baptized in the River Jordan could do so, as the Lord led. I searched my heart. I knew that God was saying he wanted me to draw a line in the sand after a recent difficult season, and that he wanted me to get baptized as a symbol of new beginnings. This time I went forward with a bit of fear and trembling. I had been involved in ministry for years and had experienced first-hand the spiritual battle against anyone trying to do something for the kingdom. By getting baptized I was declaring afresh that no matter what was to come, I was his and I would follow where he led me. Stepping into the river, I fought off the tiny fish nibbling my ankles, and emerging from the water, I cried. I knew he had forgiven me for wrongs I had done in the previous season and that he still had purpose for me, even if his original plans had gone somewhat awry in the meantime. Looking back, I realize that everything in my life began to look different from that moment onward.

He never gives up on us. Even when we want to give up on ourselves.

In those same waters two thousand years before, Jesus drew a metaphorical line as well and began his own ministry. When he emerged, all things were different and his life would literally never be the same again. That is the power of purpose. It draws us into the direction we want to go but may not know how to navigate. Even if we hit a detour along the way, purpose continues pulling us in the right direction, like a magnet to metal.

> That is the power of purpose. It draws us into the direction we want to go but may not know how to navigate.

Whose Purpose Are You Following?

It is important to remind ourselves whose purpose we are following – the Lord's or our own? Sometimes it may be difficult to distinguish between the two and often I think they are more intertwined than we think, especially if we genuinely desire to follow his will. Scripture says:

> [God] saved us and called us to a holy calling, not because of our works but because of his own purpose and grace, which he gave us in Christ Jesus before the ages began.
>
> 2 Tim. 1:9 ESV

> For he chose us in him before the creation of the world to be holy and blameless in his sight. In love he predestined us for adoption to sonship through Jesus Christ, in accordance with his pleasure and will . . .
>
> Eph. 1:4–5

> For from him and through him and for him are all things. To him be the glory for ever! Amen.
>
> Rom. 11:36

Our purpose must be outworked by giving him glory, because all things are from him, given to us through him, and are given back for him; we are ultimately here for his purposes to be outworked in our lives, to the glory of his name. And though plans come into play, and we should plan as much as we can, we must not be married to our plan above his purpose (Prov. 16:9; Jas 4:13–14). Another way to say it is to date the plan, but marry the purpose.

Jesus Christ had no will of his own; he was here solely for the purpose of fulfilling his Father's wishes and being slain for our sins. No human being, selfish desire or demonic force would stop him from carrying out his assignment on earth . . . and he was tested to a level we will never need to identify with, thankfully. In the same measure, it is only in Christ that we can keep our eyes fixed on him, our faces set like flint, and our hearts unmoved by other people's whims over God's will. Knowing him allows us to obey him.

I believe one of the greatest fears for Christians is that they will miss the will of God. For years I sought to find my purpose, fearing that I might miss it and die a life unfulfilled. The older I have

> It is not a one-time destination, but a daily lived determination.

become, the more I realize that our purpose is outworked as we live from day to day. It is not a one-time destination, but a daily lived determination. It embraces the good and the difficult, the joyful and the sorrowful, the understood and the mysterious.

As we close out this chapter, I sense some of you may need new vision over old experiences. Perhaps there was a situation in your life which you saw as purpose, but in reality it was a plan . . . and one that did not turn out as you expected. Or maybe you saw yourself at a certain place by a certain age and that has come and gone, with life looking very different from what you bargained for.

Let me redirect your attention towards purpose. In the economy of God it is never too late for purpose to unfold – notice that for Simeon and Anna it came in the latter stages of their lives. Yet, what a glorious moment that must have been for them! I imagine it made their years of waiting even more fulfilling – to be an integral part of the Messiah's story. Throughout all of our seasons, we discover purpose weaving itself in and out, like a thread of gold spun around the colours

For reflection

- God will never give up on us. How does this make you feel? Does it change the way that you see him, or your circumstances? What if we carried that same intentionality into all of our relationships . . . would we have to change the way we are behaving with some people?

- Have you ever worried about missing the will of God? If his will is not a destination, but a journey, how would you describe his will for your life?

- How can you 'reframe' a difficult circumstance in your life right now and turn it around to view it through the eyes of heaven?

- The end of the chapter talks about hearing God's voice . . . spend time in prayer, listening for him to guide you and speak to you. Enjoy his company and worship him for his goodness to you today!

20

The Impact of Influence

For if you remain silent at this time, relief and deliverance for the Jews will arise from another place, but you and your father's family will perish. And who knows but that you have come to your royal position for such a time as this?

Esth. 4:14

A Moment in Time

I think most of us who are old enough can remember where we were on 9/11, that fateful day when terrorists changed the course of history forever.

It was less than a month after this tragedy that I found myself co-leading a team of seventy students into New York City, helping where we could. Halfway through the week, I thought to myself I hadn't had my moment yet. You know, that moment which shows you why God wanted you on this particular trip. Sometimes it is for a particular child, or to pray for someone's healing, or simply to hug a stranger in a foreign country. So I asked the Lord that morning for my moment.

As the team was large, one of us needed to go early and purchase train tokens for the underground,[1] so we had them on hand for the teens before piling onto the platform. I went early to the station and filled my pockets – literally – with seventy tokens, then found a place to wait for the rest of the team. As it was raining I went for cover under a bridge near the station. It was not a particularly safe part of the city, but there were shops nearby, and a few people walking around, so I felt the risk was minimal. Not too long after, I noticed a strange man watching me. I hugged my bag a bit tighter and tried not to look as though I had $70 worth of coins in my bulging pockets. Soon he started towards me; I glanced around to see if anyone was there and realized we were now alone. As he came closer he must have sensed my trepidation because he stopped a few feet away and motioned towards his wrist: 'Time?' he questioned. He wasn't a serial killer – he didn't own a watch.

I told him the time and as he turned to walk away, for reasons still unknown to me, I stopped him and asked where he was from.

'Kosovo,' he said.

'Kosovo!' I exclaimed, then began rapidly telling him how I had been there just a few months earlier, what a lovely city, lovely people, and so forth . . . until I noticed him staring at me blankly. Clearly his English was not brilliant. Time to include hand gestures.

'Me. Kosovo,' I said (pointing at myself, then outwardly).

'You, Kosovo?' he asked, obviously understanding.

Nodding excitedly, I responded: 'Yes. Me there. Kosovo.'

'City?' he asked.

Thinking to myself that this was ridiculous as I'd only been in one city, I replied, 'Mitrovica'.

His eyes became saucers and he said, 'Mitrovica? Me . . . Mitrovica! Me!'

He was from the one city I had been in two months prior to this meeting.

It became even more bizarre.

In broken English he began describing a part of the town I recognized, by the description of the shops, and then he said, 'Bakery . . . you know the bakery?'

I did know which one he referred to, as we had walked by it several times. 'Yes . . . I know it.'

'My bakery! My bakery!' he cried.

Then he began explaining that he was stuck in the city due to 9/11 and was not able to get a flight home to see his family, including his little girl whom he deeply missed. He pulled from his pocket a picture she had coloured for him and, with tears welling up in his eyes, he simply said, 'Want to go home.' I'll never forget as he then pulled out a picture of what was clearly his extended family, all sitting in a group smiling together, and pointing to one after another he said, 'Killed in war . . . killed in war . . . killed in war . . .'

I stared, speechless. What do you say at a time like this? With tears in my eyes I asked if he knew God (and I pointed up). He made a sign of the cross. On the right track here. I pointed up and said 'God . . .' and then pointed at my eyes and said 'sees . . .' and then pointed at him. Feeling God's overwhelming love for him in my heart, I repeated this two or three times. He is seen. About that time, I heard commotion and yelling behind me: seventy teenagers were about to accost me as we were late and needed to catch the train. Soon my jacket was being pulled, my name being called and the other team leader was yelling we had to leave quickly. I only had time to hold up my hand, as the man held up his, and just before we touched

I was yanked backwards and pulled into the group of hormonal young people.

That was my moment.

Of the *thousands* of bridges in New York City, within a fifteen-minute span of time, I *happened* to be at the one where a scared, lonely man was desperate for home. And God used this American girl to remind him that God sees him, is watching over him, and in time will get him home to his family.

Only God could have orchestrated such an event, causing a reach across an ocean to happen from an encounter under a bridge.

Your Reach

You have a reach. And your reach will be different from my reach, but it is just as necessary.

We do not need more people on the platform; we need more platforms in the people. What I mean by that is we need people who carry their own platform wherever they are. It is the place from which they share the love of Christ, grace emanating off them in the super-market, or kindness shown to a hurting stranger. It is the one who embraces those of a different race and loves the person spewing hatred about his or her beliefs. We don't accept the behaviour, but we love the hurting, because for someone to walk with such hatred can only mean they have experienced hatred themselves. We are created to love; we learn to hate.

> We are created to love; we learn to hate.

We need people with platforms across the UK and all the nations of the world, looking for people to love, intentionally coming in a different spirit to the world. As I write this, there have been terrorist attacks happening in numerous countries around the world, including last week in London itself. Jesus had experience with this. At a time of Roman control in Jerusalem and Judaea, with fear rampant and soldiers freely walking around, Jesus speaks of loving your neighbour, showing this in a practical way by healing the servant of a Roman soldier (Luke 7:1–10).

Your platform is your home, town, city, business, church and bus stop. It is everywhere you put your foot and anyone on whom you rest your eyes. You have a reach. It goes further than you might think. Remember the seed we have been watching throughout the book? That promised seed of Christ has now grown in purpose and become the Saviour about to die for his reach of the world. What began as a prophecy was fulfilled in a destiny, and it is the same for you.

You have had a prophetic word over your life by the Lord, spoken before time, that you would come to be and fulfil the plans, the thoughts, he has for you. The promise may not always look far-reaching, or even monumental in purpose . . . but to the one who receives it, it is enough.

Just ask a man from Mitrovica.

Permission Granted

One of my favourite stories of Jesus reaching beyond his Jewish borders is found in Matthew 15:21–28. Here we read the story of the Syrophoenician woman:

> Leaving that place, Jesus withdrew to the region of Tyre and Sidon. A Canaanite woman from that vicinity came to him, crying out, 'Lord, Son of David, have mercy on me! My daughter is demon-possessed and suffering terribly.' Jesus did not answer

a word. So his disciples came to him and urged him, 'Send her away, for she keeps crying out after us.' He answered, 'I was sent only to the lost sheep of Israel.' The woman came and knelt before him. 'Lord, help me!' she said. He replied, 'It is not right to take the children's bread and toss it to the dogs.' 'Yes it is, Lord,' she said. 'Even the dogs eat the crumbs that fall from their master's table.' Then Jesus said to her, 'Woman, you have great faith! Your request is granted.' And her daughter was healed at that moment.

Jesus had withdrawn to that area because it was Gentile, hoping perhaps to get a time of rest with his disciples, away from their tireless schedule and constant demands from the Jewish people. Mark's account of this story makes this clear by including the detail: 'And he entered a house and did not want anyone to know, yet he could not be hidden' (Mark 7:24 ESV).

Though he was in Gentile country, his reputation still preceded him and his reach was subsequently extended beyond its intended borders – pulled out by the faith of a mother.

When a seed is planted, though we have an idea what will be produced (apples, flowers, etc.), we never know the exact look, dimensions, size and outcome of that seed. Every seed, every promise, is unique. In reality, our vision may be vastly different from God's vision, therefore holding an open hand is one of the bravest and wisest choices we could make. Never limit an unlimited God.

> Never limit an unlimited God.

When this Canaanite woman with a 'momma bear' attitude in Matthew 15 asked boldly on behalf of her little cub, Jesus' heart was moved with compassion. How could it not be? Here was a woman falling at his feet, *begging* for the life of her child, believing outside her belief system that he was the Christ, carrying power to heal. She had no doubt, only faith that he was the Anointed One . . . and she was not leaving without that healing.

Jesus answers her with words that outwardly sound cruel, by calling her a dog, yet the term he uses is actually 'little dog', as in a pet one would have in the house.[2] Though that may not seem much better, he was actually softening the term by saying she was part of the family, but in a different role from those to whom he had been called. Taking hold of his analogy, she boldly proclaimed that even the household pet was able to eat the scraps . . . She did not need much, only this one act of kindness.

Faith moves the heart of God and faith moved the compassion of his Son – her daughter was healed that instant. Imagine what would have happened if she had succumbed to the political correctness of the day which said Gentiles and Jews did not mix? Or if Jesus had been religious about his borders and refused to go beyond his stated calling?

We cannot 'box in' the will of God, nor the reach of God, in or through us. If we are willing, then he will stretch us beyond our comfort zone – every time. Because of this woman's faith, and his willingness, Jesus said to her in verse 28: 'Your request is granted.'

I love that.

Permission granted.

Faith steers the heart of God, from refusal towards permission. In other words, *boldness pulled out what boundaries kept in*. Faith goes beyond borders and puts you in positions that are off limits to others. I declare to you 'Permission granted' following the leading of the Holy Spirit on your life. Permission granted to declare healing over your family, freedom for your spouse, salvation for

> Boldness pulled out what boundaries kept in.

your children and peace in your neighbourhood. Permission granted to pray for a move of the Holy Spirit on your street, intercede for the nations, write that book, give that talk, start that business, share with that friend, buy someone that gift, and affect your nation with the love of God in small, everyday acts of kindness.

Permission granted!

Who Do You See?

When you look out of your front door, who do you see?

Jesus was there for the Jews, but he was also there for the Samaritan, the Syrophoenician and the prostitute. He found purpose in calling a woman who had been bleeding for twelve years 'daughter' and in forgiving Peter for abandoning him during his time of greatest need. It was fulfilled as he laughed with his mother and joked with his disciples. His reach went wherever he walked that day, and so does yours. Because the promise is never for us alone; it is always for those on his heart and for his kingdom.

I have alluded that as a very young child, too shy to make eye contact, I saw myself speaking around the world, impacting thousands and leaving a legacy. I still have many unfulfilled dreams, but I have travelled further than I once thought possible and have overcome insecurities I believed would never leave. The terribly – *terribly* – shy girl from a tiny rural town in southwest Michigan has already seen beyond her dreams and imaginations, and yet this is only the beginning.

Please trust me when I say that if I can do this, so can you. Regardless of your age, stage, insecurities or gifting, God can and wants to use you to spread your sphere of influence for his kingdom. You have a reach far beyond what you are currently experiencing and maybe this is the year to let go, step out, be bold and dream again. Never be satisfied with the comfortable – never. That becomes the first step towards complacency. There is a world full of people out there waiting to know they have permission to believe, to love, to fully live. And you are God's person to bring them that truth – in your own unique and God-ordained way.

As Jesus went beyond borders, creating a legacy which still speaks today, so can we.

Where will you go?

For reflection

- Where would you define your reach (sphere of influence) right now? Do you see that spreading further or into a different area(s) in the future?

- One woman pulled a healing out of Jesus that he initially seemed reticent to give (Matt. 15:21–28). When have you seen your faith pull out a victory from heaven that seemed impossible?

- *'Boldness pulled out what boundaries kept in.'* What does this sentence mean to you and your circumstances right now?

- If comfortable leads to complacency, is there any area in your life right now in danger of this happening? What could you do to stop this before you become more comfortable than God might want you to be?

Part Six

Legacy

21

It's Harvest Time

'Behold, the days are coming,' declares the LORD,
'when the plowman shall overtake the reaper and
the treader of grapes him who sows the seed'.

Amos 9:13 ESV

Perseverance Pays It Forward

I want to begin the final part of the book by honouring someone very dear to my heart. Most of you would not know her
name, but you have seen her legacy.

Elaine was my mentor for nearly sixteen years. Our relationship started when I applied for a mentor through our
local church. My application was passed to her, and though
she had decided her schedule was too full to do any further
mentoring, she chose to read it. Later she said that as she read
over what I had written, the Holy Spirit spoke to her and said
she was meant to help me. I quickly became, as she fondly
called me, one of her (many) daughters . . . and she became
my spiritual mom.

Through her I not only learned about the Lord and his ways,
but I watched how to live the Christian life well as a leader, and

as a woman. She was originally from South Africa, so I also learned the importance of stopping for a cup of tea, which helped me greatly after moving to England!

She taught me kindness, forgiveness, strength, love, compassion, worship, deep love for the Bible, faith, commitment and so much more. Another word I would liken to Elaine is 'perseverance': she would not give up, no matter how difficult the circumstances outwardly, because she had such faith in God inwardly. I saw her battle stage four cancer and win. I sat with her as she pulled her wig off, and I tried to mask my shock; but in her inimitable style she made a joke of it being like a tea cosy,[1] and I relaxed. She showed me that it was OK to talk about pain, and to trust the Lord in the midst of it.

In 2009 when life threw several 'curveballs' my way, I spent weeks with her and her husband in their home, being ministered to through their daily lives. We would talk, pray, cry, not talk, shop, play games and simply be. I could always be myself with her, knowing that I would be accepted as I was at that time in my life. I never felt disappointment from her, only love, support and belief.

It is now three years since her passing and I still well up with tears – and even cry at times – because I miss her so much. Rarely does a day go by when I don't think about her. And though you will not meet her until heaven, you feel her impact through every word written in this book. She traversed the seasons of life with me through some of my toughest times and her guidance held me to the road of integrity when I started to detour towards the danger of compromise. Watching her face her own mountains, with steely determination and a faith-filled spirit, changed my life. Even her final few texts to me were filled with faith, expressing excitement at the party to come (when she got healed) and declaring the greatness of God amid a battle which took her life less than a week after that bold declaration.

Recently I was sharing the platform with a well-known speaker, and mutual friend of Elaine, who mentioned that the ministry Elaine had helped to birth was going from strength to strength, with hundreds at a recent gathering where this speaker had been. 'She's left a great legacy,' this speaker said. Yes, she has. That is the beauty of legacy; it pays forward into the next generation seeds of wisdom from the last.

Thank you, Elaine. I will always be grateful that you navigated your promises and seasons with such grace, wisdom and perseverance, never – ever – waning in passionate love for your Saviour. It is for that reason, as I seek to fashion my own legacy, that I dedicate this book to you, and to your earthly daughter Shari, whom I have had the joy of mentoring for over twenty years.

You are forever in our hearts, our ministries and our stories.

Harvest Time

Who doesn't love a good harvest time?

After months of waiting, watering, fertilizing and praying, it is always fun to see a strong crop break forth. But every farmer, as excited as they are about the harvest, also knows this is not a season for the faint-hearted – it is the time for hard work. Proverbs 10:5 says: 'He who gathers crops in summer is a prudent son, but he who sleeps during harvest is a disgraceful son.' There is a time to rest, and harvest is not it. The Bible is very clear – we are here not for ourselves, but for his kingdom and this world. Harvest time

> Harvest time should bless us, but that blessing needs to extend beyond us for it to be a kingdom harvest which pleases God.

should bless us, but that blessing needs to extend beyond us for it to be a kingdom harvest which pleases God.

In Luke 12:48 GNT Jesus says: 'Much is required from the person to whom much is given; much more is required from the person to whom much more is given.' In a world of selfishness and 'all about me', now more than ever we must stand up and be people of a different spirit. Especially those of us in developed societies; we have a responsibility to love and care for those who are unable to care for themselves. If, at the end of my days, I have only ticked off a bucket list which benefits me, then I have not really lived; at least not according to the gospel.

So, where do you see harvest in your own life? This does not only mean financially, though that is often an indication of where our heart is when it comes to generosity. We can also harvest in our time, health, family, relationships and so much more. Grow big enough to receive a huge harvest. Because, as we have seen in previous chapters, that is what the tough seasons are for – preparation for promotion.

Hard work

'Promotion' is one of those words which sound good, but what exactly does it look like?

As we near the end of this book, let's start getting practical.

Firstly, as I have just said, the harvest season means work. It means all hands on deck. Everyone knows their position and works together in a diligent manner to bring in what is ready to be received. I remember doing this at our family's property many years ago. There were many of us working to bring in the recently cut hay before it rained. I recall it being extremely hard labour, for hours at a time, with the goal of beating both the rain and the darkness, and we (barely) made it! Thoroughly exhausted and in pain, muscles aching, hungry, sweaty and completely spent, there was a unity among all of us that was tangibly felt.

On large farms and for professional farmers, harvest season involves much more than hard work by a team for one day. But the principle is the same – no work, no harvest. We all want seasons of growth, advancement, promotion, dreams fulfilled and prayers answered, but are we ready for the work that accompanies that? A new relationship takes work, a new baby . . . (need I say more), a job promotion is challenging, getting a business off the ground can take a few years and stepping into the plans and purposes of God will always have the power of hell fighting against it. We should not shy away from any of this, but we need to go in with both our physical and spiritual eyes open; the soul-rest gained during the quiet season was in preparation for demanding work in the harvest season.

Before I go any further I need to clarify: I am not intending you to work until you are exhausted, or work from a place of striving or to gain approval from God. None of those are right, healthy or biblical. But I mean listening to the voice within, embracing the opportunities he puts in front of you; as Colossians 3:23–24 says: 'Whatever you do, work at it with all your heart, as working for the Lord, not for human masters, since you know that you will receive an inheritance from the Lord as a reward. It is the Lord Christ you are serving.'

Perhaps the new season will require some pruning – less time on social media, more time in prayer, or letting some friendships go which are not life-giving. This is not a time to become spiritually fat, but a season to walk in all that you have learned, doing all that he is asking of you, with joy, peace and a calm, yet determined, spirit.

Mind the Gap

I recently listened to a podcast where the speaker talked about helping her grandfather bring in the peach harvest when she was a child. Her job as a small 6-year-old was to stamp the crates signifying whether the peaches were of top quality or medium quality, as they divided them up between good and best. She took great pride, she explained, as a young child marking those crates the best she could. It may seem like a menial task, but it was a very important one which, if missed, could cause problems later on down the road. Each role is vital to the whole, including yours.

There is a gap somewhere in the harvest that has your name on it. It may be a person you meet at the shops who needs to know the love of a Saviour, a business partner whose failing marriage requires an extra dose of your patience, or a spouse who needs reassurance that you are committed, no matter how challenging the current season. It is a gap that only you can fill.

> There is a gap somewhere in the harvest that has your name on it.

And regardless of how menial the task might look at the moment, never despise the days of small beginnings. One act of love can save a person from making a horrible mistake, a colleague from going under, or a spouse from becoming less than their potential.

In Mark 6 we read the well-known passage about the feeding of the five thousand:

When Jesus landed and saw a large crowd, he had compassion on them, because they were like sheep without a shepherd. So he began teaching them many things.

By this time it was late in the day, so his disciples came to him. 'This is a remote place,' they said, 'and it's already very late. Send the people away so that they can go to the surrounding countryside and villages and buy themselves something to eat.'

But he answered, 'You give them something to eat.'

They said to him, 'That would take more than half a year's wages! Are we to go and spend that much on bread and give it to them to eat?'

'How many loaves do you have?' he asked. '*Go and see.*'

When they found out, they said, 'Five – and two fish.'

Mark 6:34–38[2]

We know from John 6:9 that it was a boy who gave up his five loaves and two fish in order to feed the multitude. Yet, interestingly, Jesus asked his disciples, 'How many loaves do you have?' He didn't ask them how many they could find; he asked how many they had. Possibly they had food they were saving for dinner and he was giving them an opportunity to take part in a miracle of generosity? I emphasized the phrase 'go and see' because I believe Jesus is saying the same thing to us today: will you go and see what you have to feed my kingdom?

Where is there a gap that needs filling? *Go and see.*

Where can you meet a need? *Go and see.*

For reflection

- Where are you seeing, or looking for, harvest in your own life? Where have you seen the greatest harvest in past seasons?

- No work, no harvest. So, how do we work hard for the Lord without stepping into striving and an 'earning salvation by works' mentality?

- Is there anything you sense God still needing to prune before you step into your next harvest season?

- If Jesus said to you today 'Go and see' . . . what gap would you see that needs filling?

22

The Danger of Selfishness

Whoever tries to keep their life will lose it, and
whoever loses their life will preserve it.

Luke 17:33

The Lipstick Story

Like most people, I've battled selfishness over the years. Let's be honest, we want . . . what we want! At times we are all selfish little creatures caring more about our own comfort than the comfort of others. Even as Christians we still struggle to prefer one another – getting angry if 'our' seat is taken on a Sunday morning or fighting over the last book at the book table. But on our good days, we choose blessing over battling; because God never forgets a seed of blessing sown, as I recently experienced first-hand . . .

I have a favourite lipstick, as I expect many women do. Typically I buy an expensive one each spring and autumn, making it last for the next six months, interspersing with less expensive ones when necessary. Lately I have been in a challenging season financially, so there has been no spending outside absolute necessities for many months now. One day I lost my favourite lipstick (for those who may have missed the point, this was a tragedy) and no amount of searching high and low brought me any hope – it was gone. Then, just a few hours later, I received an email from a high-end cosmetic retailer giving me a £5 voucher towards my next purchase, because 'they missed me'.

Yeah, missing you too, friend.

I looked up to heaven and said out loud, 'Lord, I would love to use that on some really nice lipstick, but I won't spend that money unless you bring it to me and make it clear I can use it for lipstick.' The next day I was speaking at a small women's meeting and after I spoke a lady came up to me and asked if we could talk.

She then said she had a strange question for me: did I need any lipstick?

After looking at her dumbfounded, I finally smiled and said, 'Well, I just lost my lipstick yesterday, so yes, I do!'

She looked relieved and said, 'When you stood up to speak, before you uttered one word, the Lord spoke to me and told me to give you £20 for a new lipstick.' And she shoved £20 into my hands.

He never forgets a seed sown. Over the years I have given several lipsticks away to friends, and now, when I needed it most, I was reaping on my seed. (As an aside, did you spot the God fingerprint?)

Don't Hoard the Harvest

I learned a big lesson that day, and not only about the faithfulness of God for even my smallest of desires; it was about having an ear to hear and a heart to obey. This woman had come to hear and receive from God, and yet she was spiritually attuned enough that God could interrupt her receiving by asking her to give. I didn't know her well, and she didn't even really know me, yet her obedience made an enormous impact on my life at a time when God was teaching me about trusting him for all of my needs.

Harvest is not only about meeting our needs, but it is about meeting the needs on his heart at that moment. And when we begin looking to give, intentionally seeking opportunities to sow, then life gets exciting. Over these past several months I have made a determination to, if possible, sow a seed every day. I have not always succeeded, but it has been my goal. Some days it was seeds of finance, other days seeds of time, gifts, encouragement or prayers . . . but each one deliberately done as an act of planting seed into the life of another. It is a joint effort with heaven, trusting when God gives me an amount to give or an assignment to do, believing that he knows more than me what he is doing behind the scenes in someone's life.

I remember last year buying lunch for a homeless woman with the last £5 in my wallet, at the time uncertain of how I would pay my rent a few weeks later. I felt the compassion of heaven for her as we talked, leaving with an empty wallet and a full heart. It may sound like a small gesture anyone would make, but I know myself and at one time, if I am honest, I would not have done it. Or I would have done it begrudgingly, thinking of my own need the entire time – about what I was losing, instead of what someone else was gaining.

Abundance is for giving – always.

Abundance is for giving – always.

Remember our parable of the sower from the beginning of the book? Before Jesus gives his explanation for the parable, he says in Matthew 13:12: 'Whoever has will be given more, and they will have an abundance. Whoever does not have, even what they have will be taken from them.' There is nothing wrong with having; in fact, we are meant to have. And those that have, and act in wisdom, will be given more. Jesus was never in want; whatever he needed his Father provided for him. He also gave, everywhere he went – food, healing, prayer, provision, wisdom, and so on. Likewise, God wants us to be his conduit of blessing today, because hoarding is not biblical.

If you struggle in this area, then I would encourage you to begin giving one thing away every day. Search your wardrobes and drawers, seeing what could bless someone else, asking the Holy Spirit to help you. Don't second-guess yourself – God will not get angry if you give away something he did not ask you to give. He is looking at the heart and the motive behind the action. Develop a habit of holding things loosely – enjoying them, not loving them.

The Invitation

Seeing people as sheep without a shepherd caused compassion to rise up in Jesus, and he said to his disciples: 'The harvest is plentiful, but the workers are few. Therefore beseech the Lord of the harvest to send out workers into His harvest' (Matt. 9:37–38 NASB).

We have seen Jesus mature from a seed-thought before time to a world-changer after birth. Receiving our promise, seeing breakthrough and experiencing a miracle are all part of the harvest season, but the real joy is in the journey, and the real journey is in the sharing. Jesus had been in ministry for about two minutes when he began calling disciples to join him, first Peter and Andrew

> The real joy is in the journey, and the real journey is in the sharing.

and then James and John, until he had a team of twelve guys eager to change the world.

I remember many years ago someone said to me, 'Jen, when you need your team, they will be there.' While there is some truth to that, and I have seen God provide miraculously in this area, there is also truth in making it happen. We must proactively look for the leaders around us, the partners in the ministry and the tribe God is calling us to join. Sitting at home praying is wonderful for a time, but at some point we must leave the sofa and pursue purpose, because purpose will never magically appear uninvited in our lives – it enjoys the pursuit. If you read John's account of the baptism of Jesus and calling of the disciples, it varies from the accounts found in Matthew, Mark and Luke. In John we see John the Baptist referring to Jesus' baptism which had happened the previous day (John 1:29–34), then we see Jesus spending time with Peter and Andrew the following day. It does not say he had already asked them to be his disciples at this time.

In fact, Andrew, Peter, John, James and Philip all lived near the Lake of Galilee and therefore had probably travelled together 80 miles to see John baptize and to learn more about this radical new rabbi.[1] This could also explain why the other gospels show Jesus getting baptized, going away into the desert for forty days to be tempted and *then* asking some of the disciples (now that he is back at the Sea of Galilee) to follow him. They quickly answered yes because they had already spent time questioning and learning from him after his baptism, then having time to ponder their conversation on the journey home.

Jesus did not wait for the guys to approach him; after spending time in prayer, *he invited them* to his work.

You may be reading this thinking you are not a leader, therefore you do not need a large team around you. That is true, you may not. But to sidestep the threat of isolation, you do need at least one other person to join you on the journey. Adam was not created to live alone, nor are we created to do life by ourselves.

If you are believing for a promise which does not involve others, then I would humbly suggest you find a new promise.

For reflection

- When have you seen God use you to bless someone else, perhaps without their knowledge? How did it make you feel?

- If you want to be a stream of giving, not a dam of possessing, how can you intentionally have 'giving goals'? Where are you currently aiming to give more?

- Who would you describe as your 'team' in life? Are you setting goals together of blessing others? If not, what would that look like if you did?

- How do your promises from God involve blessing the community and those around you?

23

The Power of Passing It On

I will surely bless you and make your descend-
ants as numerous as the stars in the sky and as
the sand on the seashore. Your descendants will
take possession of the cities of their enemies, and
through your offspring all nations on earth will
be blessed, because you have obeyed me.

Gen. 22:17–18

Life as a Pioneer

Below is an excerpt from an article I wrote for a friend's blog (edited and given with permission):

As an American I grew up learning about the pioneers, spending hours as a kid dreaming of what it would have been like to cross the country in a wagon, and at times wishing I too had lived in a little house on the prairie.

We pledged allegiance to the flag every day in school; acutely aware we were pledging allegiance to a country built on the blood and vision of those who had gone before us, enduring hardships we could never fully understand in our clean-cut, midwestern worlds. They were real pioneers, and in my mind they were untouchable legends.

I had to move 4,000 miles away to understand that one of these 'legends' lived amongst my own family.

Elizabeth Doubler was a pioneer. She was also one of the bravest women I've ever met. Barely reaching 5 ft 2 inches tall, she carried an unspoken strength and steely determination which stood her far higher than her short stature. The year 1937 saw her waving good-bye to her parents in Neustadt, Germany, at the young age of 26, calmly assuring them she would return in a few short weeks.

She never touched German soil again.

Arriving on the New York shores of America she journeyed west to Ohio, learning to speak English and securing a job as a nurse in a local hospital. (Thankfully my grandfather had tonsillitis, or I might not be typing this today!) Whilst she was falling in love and starting a family, those she left behind were falling apart and losing their families. One day her parents and brothers were at their dining room table having dinner, when there was a pounding on the door. Her parents hesitantly opened it, finding themselves eyeballing a gun held in the hands of Hitler's soldiers.

Her brothers were ordered to pack within 15 minutes, and they 'enlisted' in the army that day, never to return home as they lost their lives at war. And then post war, my great-grandparents were abruptly removed to a detention camp, as their German town suddenly became Polish. Upon their release, they returned home to find their dinner sitting on the table as they had left it . . . rotted.

Elizabeth had two remaining brothers, one on each side of the [Berlin] wall, for 30 years. Her parents ill from the camp came to live with her, as did her sister. A few strands of family ties re-united, yet the ache of separation from her brothers would never leave her. Her experience crossing the ocean was immensely different to mine. My grandmother's family was destroyed, mine as intact as when I left. She had no communication; I have instant contact day or night.

Vastly different, yet strangely similar. There was always a beautiful, unspoken understanding between us – knowing the pain of separation, yet the joy of adventure. If I've learned anything from my grandmother, I've learned to pioneer well. All of us, in our own way, are pioneers – blazing a trail for those who will come behind. We don't need a house on the prairie to bear the name pioneer and we needn't have crossed an ocean to leave a legacy of love. We simply need to live well, as my grandmother did, with conviction, faith, strength, determination, kindness, grace, and generosity.

Because real values not only cross oceans – they cross generations.[1]

Can You See It?

In the last chapter we looked at the team which helps us bring in a harvest. In this chapter we revisit the legacy we are leaving behind. As Elaine left me a legacy of mentoring and my grandmother left me a legacy of pioneering, I look now to inspire the next generation (and those following) with my own example of breaking ground for the kingdom. Pioneering is not only about moving countries; we can pioneer in our back garden. We may be the first Christian in our family lineage, the only Christian in our workplace, or the voice for the kingdom in our neighbourhood – we are a pioneer. And as such, it is our responsibility to help the next generation reach our ceiling more quickly, letting it become a floor to their future. We see this in the scripture at the beginning of the chapter. Here God spoke a legacy to Abraham before the seed of Isaac was even placed in Sarah's womb. God declared that Abraham's offspring, not Abraham, would take cities from the enemy, blessing the ends of the earth as a result. That's a legacy!

Generations were created from the seed of one man, and from your own nurtured seed of promise and purpose, many can be reached. But it is difficult to believe for what you cannot see. That is why earlier, in Genesis 15:5,

> Four vital words: *Abram believed the Lord.*

God told Abraham to go outside and look at the stars, and then he said: 'So shall your offspring be.' The next verse says: 'Abram believed the LORD, and he credited it to him as righteousness.'

Four vital words: *Abram believed the Lord.*

After seeing, he believed. How far do you see your seed of promise reaching? (You may want to pause here and ask the Holy Spirit to help you see what the Father sees.) What is the legacy you are leaving?

We must see beyond our own reach, and beyond the reach of this generation, if we are to walk with a kingdom mentality. God never saw one generation; he saw multitudes of generations to come. Jesus saw billions of people yet to come into the kingdom, not only the twelve disciples he originally chose. To walk as Jesus did we must have an eye for the one and a heart for the multitude. Perhaps you are of the younger generation reading this; it is still your responsibility to develop a heart to mentor those coming behind you. Because legacy learned early will impact others more quickly.

Go

Some of the most famous words in the Bible are found at the end of Matthew's gospel where Jesus is speaking to his, now, eleven disciples and he says:

> All authority (all power of absolute rule) in heaven and on earth has been given to Me. Go therefore and make disciples of all the nations [help the people to learn of Me, believe in Me, and obey My words], baptizing them in the name of the Father and of the Son and of the Holy Spirit, teaching them to observe everything that I have commanded you; and lo, I am with you always [remaining with you perpetually – regardless of circumstance, and on every occasion], even to the end of the age.
>
> Matt. 28:18–20 AMP

This is legacy.

Jesus took what he had (authority) and left it with his disciples (Matt. 16:19), empowering them to take his place, impacting nations beyond his own reach. Imagine that! They were going where Jesus could not reach because he was not the one to go – they were. You can reach someone I cannot reach and vice versa.

> We must see our field before we can plough it; we must know our responsibility before we can own it.

But we must see our field before we can plough it; we must know our responsibility before we can own it.

Years ago as a Missions and Outreach Pastor I was in charge of the yearly Missions Conference. We had an extremely large budget, hoping to produce a great impact over two weekends. The brief was . . . brief. They wanted my creativity, youthfulness and ingenuity to create a great conference, taking it any direction I felt led. I was terrified. *What if I made a mistake and it all went wrong?* I knew I would have to speak on the first Sunday morning in front of a few thousand people. Messing it up was all I could think about for weeks. The 'what if' will steal the 'what could be' if we allow it, and fairly quickly I might add. But God is not bothered about the 'what if' because he knows 'what could be' . . . and it is good.

I chose to persevere through my fear (terror), brought in people who knew much more than this 20-something-year-old and I prayed – without ceasing. I cannot actually remember how it all went, though I survived and didn't get fired so I am assuming it was OK, but to this day I still remember our theme. Because as I prayed, the *only* word which came to mind was this: *Go*.

One word. One command. One decision. Will you go?

At the end of the day, that is the decision we all need to make on a continual basis. Will we step out for God? Will we risk embarrassment for the reward of impact? Can we trust him to guide us through the fog and catch us if we stumble? This is what I think of when I read those two little letters. In order to leave a legacy, we must leave a location. We must step away from the familiar, wave goodbye to the comfortable and close the door behind our yesterday. It is impossible to simultaneously go and stay; one of them must bend its knee in submission to the other. Because God will never force us to do anything – ever – but he *will* give us authority, present us with opportunity and walk with us each step of the way, as Jesus did when he passed the baton to his disciples.

He made sure they knew this was not a job for a few years, but a calling for a lifetime. The period following the resurrection was not a time to ask questions about the next season; all of that was supposed to have been done in the months and years prior to this, in the seasons of hiddenness and growth. Now was the time to look outward, passing on the knowledge and gifting they had received, ensuring that the message did not die with them but lived on as an inheritance to their children's children, for generations to come.

We now hold that baton.

Jesus reassured the disciples that he was with them 'regardless of circumstance, and on every occasion'. Because even with a team around us, we can feel alone in our vision. At the end of the day we are the mother raising the children, the teacher in the classroom, the boss at work or the grandmother praying in our living room. If we are waiting to be thanked for our service, we may be waiting a while.

Leave a legacy anyway.

The Bible says: 'For the eyes of the LORD run to and fro throughout the whole earth, to give strong support to those whose heart is blameless toward him' (2 Chr. 16:9 ESV).

I believe heaven is crying out for those who will cry out on its behalf.

God is literally searching to support us. He wants to assist us in running our race, helping us leave our own set of footprints behind.

> I believe heaven is crying out for those who will cry out on its behalf.

Will we let him?

For reflection

- What is stopping you from seeing beyond your borders, so to speak? Are there any fears you need to bring to God or lay down at the Cross in order to believe for a bigger dream?

- *'To walk as Jesus did we must have an eye for the one and a heart for the multitude.'* How do you see this playing out in your own life?

- What does the word 'Go' mean to you in relation to your life right now? Where might God be asking you to go? (Remember, this does not necessarily mean you have to physically move somewhere.)

- How would you describe the footprints you are leaving behind?

24

The Life of Legacy

One generation shall praise thy works to another,
and shall declare thy mighty acts.

Ps. 145:4 KJV

The Life of Trees

At the beginning of the book I alluded to the fact (i.e. stated quite plainly) that I am not a gardener. But I am happy to say that even with limited skills around soil, I have left a legacy of trees for future generations to enjoy. Planted when I was about 10 years old, they line the quarter-mile driveway of my childhood home. My dad gave my sister and me a penny per tree, though the 'tree' at that time was a 5-inch tall wannabe. One of us would dig and the other drop, pushing soil around the edge, and on we went, along the driveway and into the surrounding fields. It felt like back-breaking work at that age, and for only a penny . . . well, the phrase 'slave labour' comes to mind!

I watched the little trees every day, bemoaning their slow growth, at times thinking what a waste of time it had been; these silly trees would never grow very large. Soon I got bored of them, spent my pennies and after another few years we moved.

Watching them as we drove out of the property, I was proud of what we had done, but I couldn't imagine Robin Hood hiding among them any time soon. I didn't give those trees any more thought for many years.

Regardless, the trees kept growing.

This past year I revisited the property for the first time in many years . . . stopping the car to gaze at the height and size of what now looked like a forest. What had been planted nearly forty years earlier, as initial seedlings, had grown to something of beauty, stature, magnificence, protection and strength.

Legacy will do that.

It takes on a life of its own, spilling beyond original borders to generations we will never meet. As a well-known Greek proverb says: 'Society grows great when old men plant trees whose shade they know they shall never sit in' (anonymous).[1]

In other words, we truly live when we do something which will have no effect on our own lives, but will forever influence the lives of future generations.

How's Your Soil Now?

The first chapter examined the substance of good soil, including a self-evaluation of our own hearts. As we begin closing out our journey of promise, we need to revisit how rich our soil is, now not only for us, but for the future generations.

The apostle Peter says (in *The Message*):

Your life is a journey you must travel with a deep consciousness of God. It cost God plenty to get you out of that dead-end, empty-headed life you grew up in. He paid with Christ's sacred blood, you know. He died like an unblemished, sacrificial lamb. And this was no afterthought. Even though it has only lately – at the end of the ages – become public knowledge, God always knew he was going to do this for you. It's because of this sacrificed Messiah, whom God then raised from the dead and glorified, that you trust God, that you know you have a future in God.

1 Pet. 1:18–21 MSG

God knows the end from the beginning and he always works with that in mind.

Before the creation of the world, Christ was chosen as a promised seed to be planted, matured, killed, and then multiplied around the world and through the ages, until the end of time. His life – his sacrifice and resurrection – was planned for our deliverance and freedom and as a type of soil into which billions of purposes have been planted, and grown, from one generation to the next.

Soil can be used by many generations. Spiritual soil breeds harvest through stories of faith, songs of hope and words of truth read for years to come; it is found in the great-great-grand-child reaping blessings from prayers sown over generations, or the children in a developing country giving their own children an education because someone sponsored them in their darkest hour. That is the soil we leave for others, and it is our responsibility to leave them untainted soil.

Unfortunately, Hezekiah was blinded to this. He was king of Judah during the prophet Isaiah's time and is best known for becoming deathly ill (Isa. 38) and being told by the prophet to put his house in order as he was about to die. After Hezekiah cried – literally – to the Lord, he was granted a life extension of fifteen years. After this the son of the Babylonian king (the enemy) sent gifts via an envoy, congratulating him on his recovery. In a not-so-bright moment Hezekiah decided to show the enemy his storehouses – all the silver, gold, spices and everything among his treasury. Only pride would do something so ridiculous, and pride became the downfall for Hezekiah's bloodline. We flirt with danger if we forget that the soil and seeds of our lives affect not only our lives, but the generations which follow us.

After this encounter, Isaiah confronted Hezekiah on what he had done, and the king readily admitted showing off all his wealth to the enemy . . . still not understanding the magnitude of his arrogant actions. Isaiah responded by saying the time would come when the storehouse goods would be carried off by the enemy and even his own future flesh and blood would be taken into captivity, becoming eunuchs in the king's palace. We might think this would have made Hezekiah sorrowful for his actions, concerned about negatively impacting his lineage, but no – not at all.

He responded by saying, "'The word of the LORD you have spoken is good" . . . For he thought, "There will be peace and security in my lifetime"' (Isa. 39:8).

In other words: 'That's OK because at least it won't be me receiving the punishment.' What selfishness! It is an arrogant attitude reflecting nothing of the kingdom, and yet how many of us have struggled at times in the same way? For example: 'As long as my family are healthy and whole, I can relax'; 'If my business is thriving and doing well, then that is my only priority'; 'I feel a bit sorry for those parents who are struggling, but at least *my* children love the Lord'; 'I'm sad about the poverty overseas, but people there should have made better choices.'

It is a subtle mindset which can sneak up on us at the most innocent of times, but it is lethal if allowed to take root in our hearts. Because that is where thoughts travel once leaving our mind . . . to our heart. And it is in our heart that they produce habits and actions. That is why the Bible is so clear that we must 'guard our heart with all diligence' (see Prov. 4:23), because it is from there that future seeds are sown and future harvest is created. Our responsibility as believers is not only to our own family, but to the family of God and to our brothers and sisters around the world. It is fine to do the best we can, pursuing excellence, walking in wealth and living in prosperity – as long as we use it for the wider world, building God's kingdom, not our own. If all believers, myself included, handled our resources with greater abandonment to his leading, I believe this world would look much different.

Hope Filled

In closing, we must leave future generations the seeds of hope, grace and kingdom-living if we want to see them mature from glory to glory, not only as individuals but also corporately as a new generation of believers.

Let's now read Romans 15:13 in *The Message*:

> Oh! May the God of green hope fill you up with joy, fill you up with peace, so that your believing lives, filled with the life-giving energy of the Holy Spirit, will brim over with hope!

The God of green hope! This is a life-giving hope produced by the life-giving energy of the Holy Spirit. He breathes hope into hopelessness and leaves the fingerprints of faith over confusion and unrest. It is something we develop and it comes out of the overflow of his presence and the Scriptures in us. Knowing his presence and understanding his word are of paramount importance for future generations to grow strong in their purpose.

We must not steal hope from those coming after us. In a world of negativity and rampant fear the church must stand up as a centre of hope, letting the world know there is something more out there than what is reported on the news. It is *our*

> Hope is a precious commodity – guard it carefully and share it freely.

responsibility to leave hope, not cynicism or sarcasm. Hope which says God is who he says he is and he will do what he says he will do.

Hope is a precious commodity – guard it carefully and share it freely.

Grace Filled

A second way we leave a strong legacy is by maximizing grace and minimizing judgment. I am quick to judge; it's part of my personality type according to the Myers-Briggs test, and I have learned that I do it quite well! I am regularly convicted by the Holy Spirit about judging others, or the situation, and more often than not I discover that I have judged incorrectly. Oh, how I am trying to improve in this area!

It is easy to see fault in the changes the next generation appear to be making, but it helps to remember we were in their shoes at one stage. Though we may (and sometimes should) wholly disagree with their actions or decisions, judgment belongs to the Lord. This does not mean we stand silent – definitely not – but we choose how best to respond, and do so with grace, love and wisdom. The Bible says that faith works by love (Gal. 5:6 ESV), so if we want to walk in faith we must walk in love. And that love is not something we have to create; it is already within us through the fruit of the Spirit.

John 1:16 in the Amplified Bible (Classic Edition) says:

For out of His fullness (abundance) we have all received [all had a share and we were all supplied with] one grace after another and spiritual blessing upon spiritual blessing and even favor upon favor and gift [heaped] upon gift.

Look at what we've been given in Christ. Grace after grace, spiritual blessing upon spiritual blessing, favour upon favour and gift heaped upon gift! My goodness, I could live off that for a while. These are ours – grace, spiritual blessing, favour and gifts – every day. Take a moment and let that sink in. Right now his grace, spiritual blessing, favour and gifts are working on our behalf and are on a collision course with our future.

> Right now his grace, spiritual blessing, favour and gifts are working on our behalf and are on a collision course with our future.

We have been given *everything* we need for life and godliness (2 Pet. 1:3); these are the tools we use to engage with the world around us today, leaving a spiritual heritage for those coming behind us tomorrow.

Kingdom Filled

And last, but definitely not least, the kingdom of God; because our lives – our promises – are for his kingdom, and his will, being done on earth, as it is in heaven (Matt. 6:10).

I remember I was overseeing the Deaf Ministry at our church years ago and often there were disputes between the hearing and the deaf over a cultural nuance, ending with one person in each camp asking me for a definitive answer over an issue. And more often than not, I would look at them both and say, 'This is not a hearing thing, nor a deaf thing – this is a kingdom thing. So, what is the kingdom answer?'

And we would come to a place of agreement because in the kingdom of God there is no hierarchy of cultures – there is no Jew or Greek, male or female – but we are all one in Christ Jesus (Gal. 3:28). And as his children we operate according to his principles, not our own prejudices or preferences. In fact, one of the greatest kingdom principles is to prefer others above ourselves . . . So that would, at times, end the argument right there!

I encourage us to look at our seeds, our promises, through kingdom eyes: the promises released for us, leaving a powerful heritage after us. Each person playing their part, contributing to God's kingdom plan, joining in this beautiful tapestry called life.

> **What part will you play?**

What part will you play?

Very truly I tell you, unless a grain of wheat falls to the ground and dies, it remains only a single seed. But if it dies, it produces many seeds.

John 12:24

'Yes indeed, it won't be long now.' GOD's Decree.

'Things are going to happen so fast your head will swim, one thing fast on the heels of the other. You won't be able to keep up. Everything will be happening at once – and everywhere you look, blessings! Blessings like wine pouring off the mountains and hills. I'll make everything right again for my people Israel:

'They'll rebuild their ruined cities.

They'll plant vineyards and drink good wine.

They'll work their gardens and eat fresh vegetables.
And I'll plant *them*, plant them on their own land.
They'll never again be uprooted from the land I've given
them.'
GOD, your God, says so.

Amos 9:13–15 MSG

For reflection

- *'Society grows great when old men plant trees whose shade they know they shall never sit in'* (anonymous). What does this quote mean to you?

- How are you intentionally leaving good soil for those who will come behind you?

- If we are meant to be 'hope givers', brimming over with hope, how can we intentionally be doing this in the lives of those we influence? Are there any areas where you are stealing hope from someone else, tearing down their dreams instead of building them up?

- What would you like your legacy to be, if it could be summed up in two or three sentences?

Author's Note

Thank you for sharing in this journey of promise with me! I pray you have been encouraged, challenged and strengthened for the exciting future ahead. God always does immeasurably more than we can imagine! (See Eph. 3:20.)

The greatest decision we could ever make in life is to follow the Lord wholeheartedly. Trusting him with our future takes courage, yet he has promised never to leave us and never to forsake us (Heb. 13:5). If you would like to become a Christian, or re-dedicate your life to Christ, please pray the following prayer with me:

Dear God,
I come to you in the name of Jesus. I admit that I have not trusted you to be my Saviour and have tried to live on my own terms. I ask you to forgive me of all my sins. The Bible says if I confess with my mouth that 'Jesus is Lord', and believe in my heart that God raised him from the dead, I will be saved (Rom. 10:9). I believe with my heart and I confess with my mouth that Jesus is the Lord and Saviour of my life from this moment forward. Thank you for saving me!
In Jesus' name I pray. Amen.

If you have prayed that prayer, I would love to celebrate with you! Please let me know by emailing your testimony to jen@jenbaker.co.uk. Also, please share with a trusted friend and find a strong Bible-teaching, Spirit-filled church to become part of, as we cannot do this journey alone.

If you would like to find out about other books I have written, please visit my website: jenbaker.co.uk.

Finally, I would love to stay in touch with you through social media. You can find me on Instagram, Facebook and Twitter here: @jenbakerinspire

Notes

1 Prepare the Soil

1 https://en.wikipedia.org/wiki/Soil#Functions_of_soils (accessed 15 Jan. 2018).
2 http://biblehub.com/greek/4073.htm (accessed 15 Jan. 2018).
3 http://biblehub.com/greek/1411.htm (accessed 15 Jan. 2018). Copyright © 1987, 2011 by Helps Ministries, Inc.

2 Beware of the Enemy

1 http://www.goodreads.com/quotes/419679-god-is-more-interested-in-your-character-than-your-comfort (accessed 15 Jan. 2018).
2 https://www.livescience.com/39461-sequoias-redwood-trees.html.
3 Conversation between the author and Sue Gibson.
4 US English: grocery store.

3 The Power of the Blessing

1 US English: dormitories.

4 Cultivating Rich Soil

[1] http://www.encyclopedia.com/earth-and-environment/ecology-and-environmentalism/environmental-studies/soils (accessed 12 Jan. 2018).

[2] http://www.encyclopedia.com/earth-and-environment/ecology-and-environmentalism/environmental-studies/soils (accessed 12 Jan. 2018).

6 The Danger of Assumption

[1] US English: shopping carts.

[2] US English: lining up.

[3] US English: coupons.

7 The Power of a Promise

[1] Emphasis mine.

[2] Emphasis mine.

[3] Emphasis mine.

[4] Smith Wigglesworth, *Ever Increasing Faith* (Springfield, MO: Gospel Publishing House, 1924), ch. 3: 'The Power of the Name', available at: http://www.worldinvisible.com/library/wigglesworth/5f00.0930/5f00.0930.c.htm (accessed 15 Jan. 2018).

8 The Merging of the Miraculous

[1] Jen Baker, *Untangled* (Farnham: CWR, 2013).

[2] http://biblehub.com/topical/b/barren.htm (accessed 15 Jan. 2018).

[3] http://biblehub.com/topical/b/barren.htm (accessed 15 Jan. 2018).

[4] US English: wrench.

[5] US English: closet.

9 The Purpose of Protection

[1] US English: flashlight.
[2] "'For I know the plans I have for you," declares the LORD, "plans to prosper you and not to harm you, plans to give you a hope and a future"' (Jer. 29:11).

10 The Danger of Doubt

[1] https://www.brainyquote.com/quotes/quotes/c/corrietenb381184 .html (accessed 15 Jan. 2018).
[2] US English: awry, horribly wrong.
[3] Adapted from George Müller's original text, available at: https:// www.allaboutfollowingjesus.org/knowing-gods-will.htm.

11 The Power of the Prophet

[1] http://www.accordingtothescriptures.org/prophecy/353-prophecies.html (accessed 15 Jan. 2018).
[2] Member of parliament.
[3] US English: mail.

12 Beauty in the Silent Years

[1] 'Wind of Change' (speech): https://en.wikipedia.org/wiki/Wind_ of_Change_ (accessed 15 Jan. 2018).
[2] http://letterinoctober.com/the-final-word (accessed 15 Jan. 2018).

13 Breakthrough on the Horizon

[1] http://www.bbc.co.uk/news/magazine-39628629 (accessed 15 Jan. 2018).

14 The Fragility of New Birth

[1] http://www.writtensound.com/index.php?term=jackhammer (accessed 15 Jan. 2018).
[2] Dutch Sheets, *Authority in Prayer* (Bloomington, MN: Bethany House, 2006), p. 20.
[3] Sheets, *Authority in Prayer*, p. 20.

15 The Power of Partnership

[1] US English: housing project.
[2] http://garden.lovetoknow.com/garden-basics/plant-growth-factors (accessed 15 Jan. 2018).
[3] Emphasis mine.

16 Seasonal Upgrade

[1] US English: railroad tie.
[2] Taken from My Utmost for His Highest® by Oswald Chambers, edited by James Reimann, © 1992 by Oswald Chambers Publications Assn., Ltd., and used by permission of Discovery House, Grand Rapids MI 4950l. All rights reserved.

17 Anointed for Purpose

[1] https://en.oxforddictionaries.com/definition/epoch (accessed 17 Jan. 2018).

[2] http://www.telegraph.co.uk/men/active/10622160/How-I-learnt-to-be-a-trapeze-artist.html (accessed 15 Jan. 2018).

18 The Danger of Giving Up

[1] https://www.goodreads.com/quotes/874355-god-never-made-a-promise-that-was-too-good-to (accessed 15 Jan. 2018).

[2] Dutch Sheets, *Intercessory Prayer* (Ventura, CA: Regal Books/Gospel Light, 1996), pp. 159, 163, 164.

19 The Power of a Purpose

[1] Stephen DeSilva, *Money and the Prosperous Soul* (Grand Rapids, MI: Chosen Books, 2010), p. 105.

20 The Impact of Influence

[1] US English: subway.

[2] https://www.gotquestions.org/Canaanite-woman-dog.html (accessed 15 Jan. 2018).

21 It's Harvest Time

[1] A padded or thick cover for a teapot to keep the tea warm.

[2] Emphasis mine.

22 The Danger of Selfishness

[1] http://www.jrtalks.com/john/john1v35to51.html (accessed 15 Jan. 2018).

23 The Power of Passing It On

[1] The full article can be read here: http://www.amyboucherpye .com/2016/04/15/ameribrit-in-london-by-jen-baker.

24 The Life of Legacy

[1] https://www.goodreads.com/quotes/666987-society-grows-great-when-old-men-plant-trees-whose-shade (accessed 15 Jan. 2018).

God Conversations

Stories of how God speaks and what happens when we listen

Tania Harris

Stories of God talking to his people abound throughout the Bible, but we usually only get the highlights. We read: 'God said "Go to Egypt,"' and then, 'Mary and Joseph left for Egypt.' We're not told how God spoke, how they knew it was him, or how they decided to act on what they'd heard.

In *God Conversations*, international speaker and pastor Tania Harris shares insights from her own story of learning to hear God's voice. You'll get to eavesdrop on some contemporary conversations with God in the light of his communication with the ancients. Part memoir, part teaching, this unique and creative collection will help you to recognize God's voice when he speaks and what happens when you do.

978-1-78078-188-4

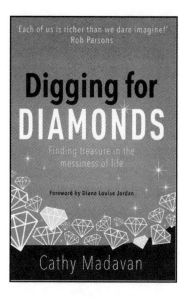

Digging for Diamonds

Finding treasure in the messiness of life

Cathy Madavan

What is hidden always shapes what we can see. In this book, Cathy Madavan encourages us to dig deeper and discover more of the life-transforming treasures of our identity, strength, character and purpose that God has already placed within us – right where we are.

Cathy explores twelve key facets which point the reader to a deeper understanding of their unique, God-given raw material and how God wants to transform them to live a valuable, purposeful life that will also unearth precious potential in others.

978-1-78078-131-0

Authentic

We trust you enjoyed reading this book from Authentic. If you want to be informed of any new titles from this author and other releases you can sign up to the Authentic newsletter by contacting us:

By post:
Authentic Media Limited
PO Box 6326
Bletchley
Milton Keynes
MK1 9GG

E-mail:
info@authenticmedia.co.uk

Follow us: